CULTURES OF THE WORLD
Iran

Cavendish
Square

New York

Published in 2015 by Cavendish Square Publishing, LLC
243 5th Avenue, Suite 136, New York, NY 10016

Copyright © 2015 by Cavendish Square Publishing, LLC

First Edition

Website: cavendishsq.com

This publication represents the opinions and views of the author based on his or her personal experience, knowledge, and research. The information in this book serves as a general guide only. The author and publisher have used their best efforts in preparing this book and disclaim liability rising directly or indirectly from the use and application of this book.

CPSIA Compliance Information: Batch #WS14CSQ

All websites were available and accurate when this book was sent to press.

Library of Congress Cataloging-in-Publication Data

Rajendra, Vijeya.
 Iran / Vijeya Rajendra, Gisela Kaplan, Rudi Rajendra.
     pages cm. — (Cultures of the world)
 Includes bibliographical references and index.
 ISBN 978-0-76144-993-5 (hardcover) ISBN 978-0-76147-993-2 (ebook)
 1. Iran—Juvenile literature. I. Besheer, Margaret. II. Spilling, Michael. III. Title.
 DS254.75.J36 2014
 955—dc23
                                    2014012957

Writers: Vijeya Rajendra/Gisela Kaplan/Rudi Rajendra; Deborah Nevins, 3rd ed.
Editorial Director, third edition: Dean Miller
Editor, third edition: Deborah Nevins
Art Director, third edition: Jeffrey Talbot
Designer, third edition: Jessica Nevins
Production Manager, third edition Jennifer Ryder-Talbot
Production Editors: Andrew Coddington and David McNamara
Picture Researcher, third edition: Jessica Nevins

Printed in the United States of America

CONTENTS

IRAN TODAY

I**T'S NOT HARD TO FIND IRAN ON A MAP OF ASIA. THE ALASKA-SIZED NATION** lies in the heart of central Asia, bordering the Gulf of Oman, the Persian Gulf, and the Caspian Sea. Seven other Asian countries border Iran: Iraq, Turkey, Armenia, Azerbaijan, Turkmenistan, Afghanistan, and Pakistan.

It is a land of spectacular beauty, with windswept deserts, rock formations spouting water springs, pomegranate orchards, pistachio orchards, rows of stately Lombardy poplars, and extinct volcanoes. The country is still dotted with the camps of nomads who have traversed Iran's central plateau for time immemorial. Iran's coastline on the Caspian Sea is rated among the world's most beautiful, with mountains rising above turquoise waters. Modern Iran is a mix of old and new, with the congested traffic of Tehran, vast oil fields in the south, the dusty remains of great empires, and some of the world's most beautiful buildings.

In the latter part of the twentieth century, however, the image of Iran that most Americans became familiar with was not so beautiful. TV news images regularly showed crowds of Iranians chanting slogans such as "Death to America," and "America the Great Satan." American leaders, in turn, characterized Iran as part of

Iranian students burn a portrait of U.S. president Barack Obama during a demonstration outside the former U.S. embassy in Tehran in 2009.

an "Axis of Evil." Repeatedly, Iranian leaders have called for the destruction of Israel, America's chief ally in the Middle East. Since the overthrow of the shah, or king, of Iran in 1979 by Iran's "Islamic Revolution," the United States and Iran have had no diplomatic relations.

LIFE IN THE ISLAMIC REPUBLIC

Officially, Iran today is an "Islamic Republic," a country run by Islamic law under a 1979 Islamic constitution. Security forces in Iran patrol the streets to make sure that people are following religious laws, which instruct them in how to dress and behave. Pop and rock music from the West are forbidden because religious authorities think such music leads people away from Islam. Dancing is considered sinful. Smoking or drinking alcoholic beverages is strictly punished. Kissing in public can bring a punishment of one hundred lashes with a whip.

Even though Iran's constitution guarantees freedom of speech, there is little such freedom as Americans know it. The role of Iran's newspapers, radio, and television in Iran is to support Islam and Islamic culture as Iran's clerical leaders see it.

Islamic law in Iran stresses that women must pursue traditional roles as wives and mothers. The shah, when he was in power, had abolished dress restrictions for women. With the establishment of the Islamic Republic, however, women were once again required to wear the *hijab*—modest loose clothing that exposes only the hands and face. A woman wearing improper clothing in public—perhaps exposing too much of her arm or hair—faces fines, lashes with a whip, and even imprisonment.

While women's rights have taken a step backward in Iran, there has been some progress. Women are now allowed to get the same education as men. Their job opportunities have increased. Unlike women in Saudi Arabia, a very strict Islamic nation, women in Iran can drive cars and run their

A trader speaks on her phone on the floor of the Tehran Stock Exchange in 2013.

own businesses. In recent years, more Iranian girls than boys have passed university entrance examinations.

Many people in Iran today believe that restrictions on personal freedom should be further loosened. These people are called *reformists*. They are opposed by religious conservatives who want to keep a very strict interpretation of Islamic law. In 1999, Iran was rocked by serious unrest as reformist students staged protests across the nation. The student revolt was crushed by the government, which jailed many and shut down their publications. The government also banned political parties that called for reform and closed newspapers and magazines that printed antigovernment articles.

Tensions today between Iran and the West, especially the United States, remain very high, but may be slowly easing. Relations plunged into the deep freeze in 2002, when U.S. spy satellites photographed uranium-enrichment plants that Iran's government had not reported to the International Atomic Energy Agency (IAEA), a U.N. organization that monitors the spread of nuclear weapons.

The element uranium needs to go through an enrichment process in order to be used in power plants and in making nuclear weapons. Confronted with this evidence, Iran's government admitted that it had hidden a uranium enrichment program from the world for eighteen years. Today, Iran continues to enrich uranium openly in defiance of the United Nations.

Building a nuclear weapon, says the United States and its allies, means that Iran is deliberately violating the Nuclear Nonproliferation Treaty (NPT). The NPT was originally signed in 1968 and has since been renewed several times. Under its provisions, nations with nuclear weapons at the time—the United States, the Soviet Union, China, the United Kingdom, and France— agreed not to give nuclear weapons, or the means to build them, to other nations. Any non-nuclear nation that signed the treaty agreed not to build nuclear weapons. Iran is one of the 187 nations that have signed the NPT.

The United States and its allies worry that a nuclear-armed Iran could throw the entire Middle East into turmoil. Other countries in the region would be tempted to build their own nuclear weapons in response and the world would be drawn closer to the prospect of nuclear war. Iranian leaders then and still today strongly deny charges that they want to build nuclear weapons but rather that they are pursuing a uranium enrichment program only to build nuclear power plants.

Today Iran remains under international sanctions barring it from importing or exporting nuclear material or know-how. The U.S. and other nations have also placed sanctions imposing restrictions on trade and international banking with Iran. The sanctions have seriously hurt Iran's economy. The U.S. sanctions prohibit almost all trade with Iran, making some exceptions for activity "intended to benefit the Iranian people," including the export of medical and farm equipment, humanitarian assistance, and trade and "informational" material such as films.

After years of an increasingly tense standoff with western nations, on November 24, 2013, Iran agreed to curb its uranium enrichment activities. In return the United States and other nations agreed to ease up on the sanctions that have so hurt Iran's economy. The agreement, however, is only an interim, or temporary, agreement and all parties agree that a more permanent agreement is needed if tensions in the Middle East are to be seriously eased.

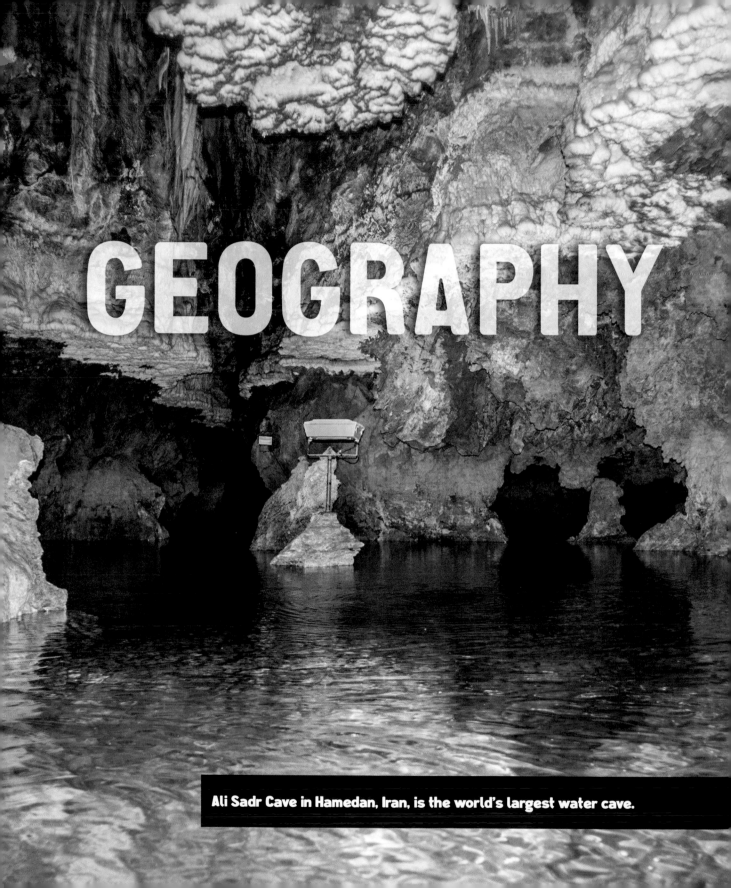

GEOGRAPHY

Ali Sadr Cave in Hamedan, Iran, is the world's largest water cave.

1

RAN IS THE EIGHTEENTH-LARGEST country in the world, with 636,000 square miles of mountains, deserts, grasslands, and forests. It is a country of great natural diversity, spectacular landscapes, and climatic extremes. It has one of the world's largest crude oil reserves in the south by the Persian Gulf. In the north lies the Caspian Sea, the world's largest lake.

Hormuz Island, a ruggedly beautiful but mostly barren island, lies off the coast of Iran in the Strait of Hormuz in the Persian Gulf.

Iran is particularly susceptible to earthquakes. The Iranian plateau is crossed by several major fault lines, which cause volcanic eruptions as well as frequent earthquakes. The most devastating earthquake in recent history, in terms of lives lost, took place Dec. 26, 2003, in the city of Bam.

Extinct volcanoes create distinctive ponds such as this one near Damavand Mountain in Iran.

LAND OF MOUNTAINS

A combination of volcanic cones, jagged mountains, lofty peaks, and barren deserts makes for a unique landscape. Iran's tallest mountain is Damavand, with a snow-covered peak all year round. So majestic in appearance is Damavand that early Iranians told tales of heroes and demons who lived on the mountain. Other volcanoes in Iran include the 12,162-foot-tall (3,707-m-tall) Sahand and the 12,805-foot-tall (3,903-m-tall) Lesser Ararat.

Located in a major seismic belt, Iran has suffered many devastating earthquakes. The country is blessed with natural resources, including petroleum and natural gas.

Copper is one of the most important minerals in Iran. Two of the country's largest copper mines are Miduk and Sarcheshmeh, both in the province of Kermanshah. Iran's deserts have plentiful supplies of salt. Other minerals found in Iran include asbestos, chromium, gold, iron ore, lead, manganese, sulfur, tungsten, turquoise, uranium, and zinc.

Rising around 3,000 to 5,000 feet (914 to 1,524 m) above sea level, the Iranian plateau dominates much of the country's interior. The Iranian plateau is almost surrounded by mountain ranges—to the west lie the Zagros Mountains, Iran's longest range, and to the north lie the Alborz Mountains, which includes the highest peak in the country, Mount Damavand.

RIVERS

Iran's main navigable river is the 450-mile-long (724-km-long) Karun. Its source is in the Zagros Mountains. The Karun River empties into the Persian Gulf through the 120-mile-long (193-km-long) Shatt al-Arab, a tidal river formed by the confluence of the Euphrates and Tigris rivers in neighboring Iraq. The Shatt al-Arab forms part of the border between Iran and Iraq.

An Iranian border post is seen from the other side of the Karun River, near the border of Iran and Iraq.

There are four main drainage basins in Iran: the Caspian Sea; the Persian Gulf; the two great deserts, Dasht-e Kavir and Dasht-e Lut; and the largest lake completely within Iran, Daryacheh-ye Orumiyeh. In winter streams bring water to the deserts and form salt lakes, but these dry up in summer.

SCARCITY OF WATER

Salt lakes are a prominent feature of Iran's desert landscape. There are two kinds of salt lakes: a *kavir* (KEH-veer) is an often dangerous salt marsh, while a *namak* (NAH-mahk) is usually shallow and has less mud. The salt in these lakes shines with a blinding brightness in the harsh Iranian sun.

The Kavir Buzurg, or Great Kavir, and other salt lakes in the Dasht-e Kavir have characteristics similar to quicksand, making the desert a dangerous terrain for inexperienced travelers.

Freshwater lakes are rare in Iran. To bring water to drier areas, early Iranians developed a clever system of irrigation. By building a long tunnel called

Salt lakes shine brilliantly in the hot desert sun. Salt lakes are far more common than fresh lakes in Iran.

a *qanat* (kah-NUT) deep in the ground, they could transport underground water to a dry area. A network of such tunnels made it possible to cultivate land that was previously too dry to farm. Qanat networks are also used to channel water from the valleys to the villages and fields. The qanat method is still used to irrigate desert land, not only in Iran, but in other Middle Eastern nations such as Oman.

Another solution to the scarcity of water in Iran is the construction of dams. This technique dates back to the time of the early Iranians. Dikes that are hundreds of years old have been discovered in Khorasan province.

More recently, the Iranian government has built a number of large dams; the largest is the Karun III on the Karun River. The seventh-largest dam in the world, the Karun III stands at a height of 673 feet (205 m). Besides providing water for irrigation, dams also supply fresh water and generate electricity for the cities.

The Karun III hydroelectric dam on the Karun River in the province of Khuzestan was built in a narrow, rocky gorge to control flooding and produce electric power.

CLIMATE

Iran is a land of extreme climates, with hot summers and cold winters in most parts of the country. Days can get very hot, while night temperatures can plunge. Iran's sheltered location in a vast landmass and its encircling mountain ranges shut out the moderating influence of the ocean.

Most of Iran's rainfall occurs during the winter months, between November and April, and rains are usually light showers. Iran's most watered parts are in the north and west. The Caspian Sea coast is the only place where there is sufficient rainfall to farm without irrigation.

The rest of the country receives very little rain annually: about 12 inches (30.5 cm) in the Iranian plateau and 5 inches (12.7 cm) in the desert lands covering most of the country. The skies over Iran are usually clear and cloudless for lack of moisture.

Temperatures in Tehran range from 27°F to 45°F (-2.8°C to 7.2°C) in January, the coldest month, and from 72°F to 99°F (22.2°C to 37.2°C) in July,

Snowfall can be heavy in the Alborz Mountains in northern Iran. The mountains rise up from the coastal region of the Caspian Sea.

the hottest month. Frost is common during winter, and snow covers the mountain peaks most of the year. Melting snow is another source of water for agriculture and personal consumption.

IRAN'S FLORA

Iran's vegetation reflects the country's climate and its position between Asia and Africa. Shrubs and thorn plants are common in Iran, where 75 percent of the land is arid or semi-arid. Many of these shrubs are either spiny or prickly to reduce the loss of moisture. In the salt regions, plants are resistant to both salt and drought.

Iranian shrubs produce a variety of useful substances, such as gum, licorice, and camel's thorn, which yields Persian manna. Poppy, sesame, tamarind, and tarragon lend flavor to food, while henna, indigo, and saffron

Wildflowers sprout up among the ruins of Persepolis.

The Persian leopard is an endangered species native to Iran. The small population that remains lives mostly in the forests, meadows, and rugged areas of the Alborz and Zagros mountains in the northern part of the country.

are traditional coloring agents.

A wide range of herbs thrives at higher elevations. The slopes of the Zagros consist mainly of grasslands and woodlands, and wildflowers bloom in spring. Wildflowers in Iran include buttercups, geraniums, gladioli, irises, orchids, and roses, the country's most popular flower, beautifully represented in paintings and carpet designs.

The Caspian and Zagros forests are populated by shrubs, ferns, and trees such as elm, maple, oak, walnut, pear, plum, and pistachio. (The export of pistachio nuts is an important contributor to Iran's economy.) Juniper, almond, and fruit trees grow in the plateau area, while the oases support date palms, acacia, poplar, and willow trees.

IRAN'S FAUNA

Iran is home to a wide variety of wild animals. Zagros mountain fauna include brown and black bears, foxes, Persian squirrels, and gazelles. Caspian forest fauna include red and roe deer, wild pigs, and tigers. Panthers still roam many areas of Iran, and there are small populations of cheetahs and leopards. Other wild animals include hedgehogs, hyenas, ibex, jackals, rabbits, wolves, and wild asses, goats, and sheep.

Species of birds found in Iran include eagles, partridges, pelicans, pheasants, shrikes, sparrows, and vultures. Ducks, geese, and seagulls populate the coastal areas in the north and south of the country. Other birds living in or passing through Iran include flamingos, kingfishers, nightjars, swallows, swans, and woodpeckers.

Iran has a variety of marine life, with around 200 species of fish.

Lobsters and turtles live in the Persian Gulf, while beluga and Iranian sturgeon swim in the Caspian Sea. (Sturgeon eggs, or caviar, are an important source of export revenue for Iran.) Otters swim the rivers of the Zagros Mountains, and trout live in abundance in the mountain streams. Iran's waterways also support large populations of herring, mullet, salmon, and tuna.

INTERNET LINKS

travel.nationalgeographic.com/travel/countries/iran-guide
National Geographic overview of Iran.

www.worldatlas.com/webimage/countrys/asia/ir.htm
World Atlas has good maps and sections on Iran's geography.

HISTORY

The Tomb of Cyrus the Great dates to around 500 BCE.

2

RANIANS ARE PROUD OF THEIR history, which goes back 5,000 years. It is a history of epic battles, mighty empires, and great accomplishments in science, art, and literature. Although a quick overview makes it appear as if Iran's history is simply a long series of one group overthrowing another—and indeed it is just that—each chapter is its own fascinating tale. Iran's story is filled with some of history's most intriguing characters, such as Alexander the Great, Omar Khayyam, Ghengis Khan, and Marco Polo. These larger-than-life heroes and villains still captivate the world's attention today.

ANCIENT IRAN

Archaeologists have evidence that humans were living in what is now Iran more than 100,000 years ago. A people called the Elamites established the first cities in southwestern Iran around 3000 BCE. Some scholars think that the Elamites originally came from what is now India.

The famous traveler Marco Polo journeyed through Persia on his expedition from Venice to China. Along the way, he and his contingent traveled the Silk Road, a network of trade routes linking Europe and Asia. Polo's voyage, which began in 1271, took three years. He returned to Venice in 1295 with jewels, spices, and a bounty of fabulous stories.

Beginning about 1500 BCE, new groups of people began migrating into Iran from the plains of Central Asia. These people are now called Aryans (AIR-e-ans). The name *Iran* comes from the ancient Persian word *Aryanam*, which means "Land of the Aryans."

CYRUS THE GREAT

By the 900s BCE, two major groups of Aryans occupied much of Iran: the Medes and the Persians. The Persians took their name from Parsua (par-SOO-uh), a region in southwestern Iran where most of them lived. At first, the Persians were dominated by the Medes, who had built a powerful kingdom in western Iran. By 550 BCE, however, a remarkable leader emerged among the Persians. He was Kurash (KOOR-ash), or Cyrus.

Cyrus organized a powerful Persian army. By 539 BCE, Cyrus had conquered vast areas of land, including the empire of Babylon, and much of what is now

A carving in the side of a cliff in Shiraz depicts the palace of Xerxes.

The ancient Persians practiced Zoroastrianism, a religion that, according to legend, began with a Persian prophet, or wise man, named Zoroaster (zohr-o-AS-ter). Zoroaster reportedly lived in eastern Iran between 628 BCE and 551 BCE, but no one is certain.

When he was thirty years old, Zoroaster said he received a vision from a divine power called Ahura-Mazda. The vision revealed a universal battle between Ahura-Mazda, the god of light, and Angra Mainyu, the spirit of evil. According to Zoroaster, all humans must choose between good (Ahura-Mazda) and evil (Angra Mainyu). Those who chose Ahura-Mazda helped the poor, told the truth, and generally tried to make the world a better place. Those who were boastful, greedy, and selfish aligned themselves with Angra Mainyu. Zoroaster taught that there would come a judgment day when Ahura-Mazda would finally defeat Angra Mainyu. On that day the followers of good would gain eternal life and the followers of evil would endure eternal pain.

The teachings of Zoroaster are written down in the Zend-Avesta, the Zoroastrian holy book. For centuries, Zoroastrianism was the state religion of the Achaemenid, Parthian, and Sassanian empires. Zoroastrian clergymen, or magi, are widely believed to be the three wise men at the nativity of Jesus.

Scholars believe that the ideas of Zoroastrianism deeply influenced other religions in the Middle East, including Christianity. Zoroastrianism is still practiced today by some people in Iran and in India, where they are known as Parsis. Like Christians and Jews, Zoroastrians are recognized as an official religious minority in Iran, where they number about 20,000 today.

Iraq, Syria, and Turkey. (The Bible's Old Testament hails Cyrus as the liberator of Jews who had been held captive by the Babylonians.)

Cyrus was the founder of the Persian Achaemenid (ah-KEE-me-nid) Empire—an empire that became the greatest world power up until that time. When Cyrus was killed in 530 BCE, his son Cambyses took the throne. Cambyses expanded the Achaemenid Empire by conquering Egypt, Afghanistan, and parts of India. The empire stretched all the way west to the border of present-day Libya in the south and up to Greece in the northwest. Darius I (ruled 521 BCE to 486 BCE) and Xerxes (ZERK-ses) (ruled 486-465 BCE) further expanded and strengthened the empire.

About forty-four miles north of the modern Iranian city of Shiraz lies the magnificent ruins of Persepolis, the ceremonial capital of the Achaemenid Empire. Archaeological evidence indicates that the remains of Persepolis date from around 515 BCE. Historians think Cyrus the Great picked the site for the soon-to-be great city, and construction began under the rule of King Darius the Great, who reigned from 522 to 486 BCE. His successors carried on the task for many years.

Among the colossal buildings at Persepolis were military barracks, the treasury, and reception halls and houses for the king. Xerxes the Great had the Gate of All Nations built at Persepolis. It consisted of a grand hall 82 feet (25 m.) in length. A pair of lamassus, *bulls with heads of bearded men, stand by the hall's western entrance. Another sculptured pair and a depiction of Xerxes stands by the eastern entrance, designed to reflect the empire's power. Xerxes's name was written in three languages and carved at the entrances. At special times during the year, representatives from all the nations ruled by the Persians came to Persepolis to present gifts of tribute to the ruler, who was known as the "king of kings." In 330 BCE, Alexander the Great's army captured Persepolis, looted it, and burned the city down. The Greek historian Plutarch reported that Alexander carried away the treasures of Persepolis on the backs of 20,000 mules and 5,000 camels.*

The Achaemenid Empire was the world's superpower of the time. The Persian army and navy were unable to defeat the Greeks, however. The Persians were driven back from their attempted conquest of Greece by numerically inferior Greeks at Marathon in 490 BCE and the sea battle at Salamis in 480 BCE. The Achaemenid Empire came to an end when Alexander

the Great defeated Darius III (c. 380—330 BCE) in a series of battles before capturing the Achaemenid capital of Persepolis in 330 BCE.

Only twenty years old when he became king of Macedonia, Alexander set out to conquer first Greece, then Persia with great enthusiasm. He won all his battles. He introduced Greek culture and political structure in Persian lands, and many Greek soldiers settled there. Alexander respected the Persian aristocracy and chose young Persians to train for his army. He tried to unite the Persians and the Greeks through intermarriage. He himself married a Persian princess, Roxana of Sogdiana, and encouraged his generals to marry the daughters of Persian nobles.

Alexander accomplished all that before the age of 32, when he died in 323 BCE. He left no heir to his vast empire, and his generals fought for control. One of them, Seleucus, finally won, and he founded the Seleucid Dynasty.

But unlike Alexander, the Seleucids were not popular among the Persian nobility. They also faced rebellions by the nomads, who fought with the settled people.

Excavated fragments of Iran's ancient history stand in Persepolis.

HERODOTUS THE HISTORIAN

Much of what we know today about Cyrus and Darius comes from the Greek historian Herodotus (her-AH-do-tus). He lived from 484 to 425 BCE. He traveled widely throughout Greece, Egypt, and parts of the Persian Empire. He is still celebrated today

for his objectivity, for being even-handed in his treatment of both Greeks and non-Greeks in his historical reporting. Herodotus has been called "the father of history," and "the first historian." Around 425 BCE, he published his main work, called The Histories, *an account of the Greco-Persian Wars (499–479 BCE.) The Greek word* historie *means "inquiry," and it is from his work that the modern meaning of the word* history *emerged.*

Herodotus was the first historian known to collect his materials in an organized way and arrange them in a story that people could easily read. He also, in his travels, collected fables, legends, and outright gossip, and included those in his history as well, leading some critics to call him "the first liar." Nevertheless, Herodotus shed great light on an era of Persian history and invented a whole new genre in the process.

THE PARTHIAN KINGDOM

Migration of Iranian peoples such as the Yüeh-chih and the Parni contributed to the decline of Seleucid rule in Iran. Parni nomads from northern Iran invaded the Seleucid province of Parthia southeast of the Caspian Sea. They established an indigenous Parthian kingdom, with their chief, Arsaces, as king, in about 250 BCE.

Future Parthian rulers extended their kingdom to include lands from Armenia to present-day Pakistan. Parthian rule lasted around 500 years, until a new Persian dynasty arose.

THE SASSANIAN DYNASTY

In 224 CE Ardashir I, ruler of a Persian state in the province of Fars, declared war against the Parthian king Artabanus V. Ardashir defeated Artabanus, ending the Arsacid dynasty of the Parthians and founding the Sassanian Dynasty of the Persians.

The Sassanids established Zoroastrianism as the official state religion and founded or rebuilt many cities and dug canals and built bridges. Architecture from the Sassanian era includes many Zoroastrian fire temples and the palace of Ardashir I in Fars province.

Ardashir, claiming the title "king of kings," actively expanded the empire and established the city of Ctesiphon in present-day Iraq as the Sassanid capital. Ardashir's son, Shapur I, and future Sassanid emperors continued to defend and expand the empire, even in the face of wars with the Romans.

In the early 600s King Khosrow II reached Chalcedon, near Constantinople (present-day Istanbul), the capital of the Byzantine Empire. The Byzantine emperor Heraclius fought back and defeated Khosrow, and the Persians lost the western territories they had conquered.

The Zoroastrians didn't bury their dead. Instead they laid the corpses in the open inside a cylindrical Tower of Silence atop a hill or mountain. There vultures would feed on the corpses, and the remaining bones would bleach in the hot sun.

THE COMING OF ISLAM

In 632 CE, the Sassanids were wiped out when Arab armies, inspired by the new religion of Islam, swept out of the Arabian Peninsula and conquered country after country. An Arab army took over what is now Iraq, defeating the Sassanids, then advanced into Iran and defeated the main Sassanid army at the battle of Kadisiyah (kad-e-SIGH-yah) in 635. Ctesiphon fell in 637. In the next few years, all of Iran became part of the Arab Muslim empire and gradually most Iranians converted to the new religion of Islam. Iran's legal system was now based on the Qur'an, the Muslim holy book.

Under Islam, Persian culture bloomed. Poets, scientists, and mathematicians flourished. Omar Khayyam (Omar the tentmaker), who lived from 1048 to 1131, is a cultural hero to many Iranians today. He was a famous astronomer and mathematician. He is also famous for writing a collection of Persian poems, called *rubyiats*.

Omar Khayyam is one of the most celebrated of Iran's poets.

For more than 600 years under Muslim rule, Persian culture became popular and widespread. Europeans began to study Persian science and appreciate Persian arts—literature, music, painting, and carpets.

MONGOL ATTACKS

In the 1200s, Mongol armies from what is now Mongolia, led by Genghis Khan, conquered and burned Iran's cities, killing hundreds of thousands of people. These murderous invaders spread destruction and terror from northern China through Persia across the Middle East and north into Russia—creating, in the process, the huge Mongol Empire. Genghis Khan's grandson, Hulagu Khan, founded the Il-Khan Dynasty in Persia in 1256, and made the Iranian city of Tabriz his capital. The Il-Khanids ruled a vast territory that included present-day Iran, Iraq, parts of present-day Russia, and Turkey for the next 200 years.

SHAH ABBAS THE GREAT

In 1501 the Safavids, a Turkish people, took control of Iran. Under Shah (King) Abbas the Great (1588—1629), Persian culture again flourished and Iran grew powerful again. He reorganized the Persian army and made alliances with European nations.

Persian architecture reached new heights of beauty under the shah's patronage. He built the magnificent capital city of Isfahan, which gave rise to the saying *"Esphahan nesf-e-jehan"* (ES-FAH-hahn nesf-je-hahn), meaning "Isfahan is half of the world." Travelers to Persia from the court of England's Queen Elizabeth I went back home with glowing accounts of Persia's splendor.

The Safavid Dynasty fell when Afghans invaded Iran and captured Isfahan in 1722. However, the Afghan interlude was short-lived. A Turk, Nader Shah (1736—47), assembled his own navy and built a large army. Nader Shah not only drove out the Afghans and reunited Iran, but later went on to conquer Afghanistan itself. Faced with a lack of money, Nader Shah decided to invade Delhi in India and bring back India's Mughal emperor's precious stones and jewelry. The loot helped Nader Shah to finance his empire, without imposing new taxes in Iran.

Sheikh Lotfollah Mosque in Isfahan dates to the early 1600s.

In 1747 Nader Shah was assassinated, and his army fell apart, with commanders aiming to set up their own states. Civil war between rival factions—the Zands and the Qajars—followed.

THE QAJAR DYNASTY

The Qajar leader Agha Muhammad Khan defeated the Zands and crowned himself the first king of the Qajar Dynasty in 1796 only to be murdered in less than a year. In 1797 his nephew Fath-Ali Shah took the throne.

During the nineteenth century, Iran found itself reluctantly involved in the political quarrels and colonial intrigues of Europe. Iran's strategic location was part of the problem. It lay between two rival nations: Great Britain and Russia. Russia, whose ports were frozen in winter, was anxious to gain entry to the warm waters of the Caspian Sea, whereas Great Britain was on alert for any threat to the most important part of its empire—India.

The Qajar rulers needed money badly and granted concessions to Russia and Great Britain in return for loans. The conditions of the loans gave these two powers a lot of control over Iran's internal affairs.

As a result, many Iranians came into contact with the Western world during the Qajar era. Europeans came to Iran to construct more modern roads, bridges, and other infrastructures. Their presence was controversial because they did not always respect local traditions or values. But this exposure to Western ideas also introduced the concept of political freedom to Iran, and in 1906 the shah was forced to proclaim a constitution.

During World War I, despite appeals to respect its neutrality, Iran was occupied by British and Russian troops. In 1921 an Iranian officer, Reza Khan, took control of the Iranian military, and in 1925 he deposed the last Qajar king. In 1926 Reza Khan founded the Pahlavi Dynasty.

Shah Reza Khan Pahlavi in 1938

THE PAHLAVI DYNASTY

Reza Shah Pahlavi set out to modernize and Westernize Iran through many reforms. He introduced civil law, established the first national bank, modified divorce law in favor of women, and prohibited women from wearing a veil. He also sought independence from foreign interference. The name of the country was officially changed from Persia to Iran in 1935.

During World War II, owing to Iran's ties with Nazi Germany and its policy of neutrality, the shah refused to expel Germans from Iran and denied Allied forces passage through Iran. Needing to transport U.S. war supplies to the Soviet Union through Iran, British and Soviet forces invaded Iran in 1941, forcing the shah to leave. He was succeeded by his son, Muhammad Reza Pahlavi (pah-LAH-vee).

Shah Muhammad Reza Pahlavi, son of the first shah, is shown in the 1950s.

Faced with the task of restoring the country, the new shah set out to redistribute land, reduce illiteracy, and build industry. Opposition to his pro-Western rule grew intense, however, as people organized anti-shah groups and wrote articles attacking government corruption and the shah's excessive lifestyle.

The new shah allowed British and American companies to continue to run Iran's valuable oil industry. In the early 1950s, a strong movement grew in Iran to have the Iranian government take over the oil industry. This movement was led by Premier Muhammad Mossadeq. On August 16, 1953, Mossadeq, with the overwhelming support of the Iranian people, was elected as prime minister. He forced the new shah into exile and nationalized the oil industry. The shah, however, returned to his throne three days later when a coup organized by the British MI6 (Britain's foreign intelligence service) and the American CIA deposed Mossadeq. The shah gave control of the oil fields back to British and American companies. Mossadeq was arrested and imprisoned for the remainder of his life.

AN ISLAMIC REPUBLIC

During Muhammad Reza Shah's reign, Iran became increasingly Westernized, but many Iranians considered this transformation an insult to the traditional values of Islam. Rapid industrialization also meant ballooning populations in the cities, resulting in social problems.

The angry Iranian people gave their support to Ayatollah Ruhollah Khomeini, a religious leader in exile since his arrest in 1963. *Ayatollah* is a Persian word meaning "Sign of God." Widespread civil unrest brought down Iran's monarchy in January 1979.

Ayatollah Khomeini then returned to Iran and proclaimed it an Islamic republic. He declared an end to Western influences in Iran, and those who broke the fundamentalist Islamic social codes were caught by patrolling revolutionaries and severely punished. Many foreign-educated upper- and middle-class Iranians fled the country and settled overseas. The new regime also carried out a brutal campaign to eliminate political opponents.

In November 1979, after the exiled shah went to the United States for cancer treatment, the Ayatollah's supporters took more than sixty Americans hostage at the U.S. embassy in Tehran. The shah died in exile in 1980. The hostages were not freed until January 1981.

Ayatollah Ruhallah Khomeini led the Islamic Revolution in 1979.

WAR WITH IRAQ

Border disputes have long been a source of tension between Iran and Iraq. Religious differences also played a role. Iraqi dictator Saddam Hussein and his supporters were Sunni Muslims, whereas much of Iran belongs to the Shia branch of Islam.

In 1980, when internal political problems weakened Iran, Hussein's Iraqi regime saw a chance to attack and tried to seize Iran's oil-producing province of Khuzestan. The Iranian army put up a surprising defense, and throughout the war both sides suffered massive losses, especially in population centers and at oil refineries. The Iran-Iraq war ended in 1988, with a UN resolution for a mutual ceasefire.

In 1989 Ayatollah Khomeini died of a heart attack. As the nation mourned Khomeini's death, Iran's president, Ali Khamenei, was chosen to be the next ayatollah. Hashemi Rafsanjani replaced Ali Khamenei as president.

Rafsanjani's presidency marked the start of a more progressive and pragmatic era in Iran's recent history, especially in trade and foreign policy. In 1990 Iran resumed diplomatic relations with Great Britain. This paved the way toward mending ties with other Western nations, which would bring sorely needed foreign investment to rebuild Iran's war damage.

Iranian soldiers run from a blast in the southern part of the country during the Iran-Iraq War.

Former Iranian president Mahmoud Ahmadinejad visits a uranium enrichment facility in 2008.

IRAN DEFIES THE WEST

After 2002, however, when the controversy over Iran's nuclear program was born, relations between Iran and the West took a major downturn. In 2005, Tehran's conservative mayor, Mahmoud Ahmadinejad, was elected president, replacing Rafsanjani. Ahmadinejad almost immediately became a very controversial leader. He hardened Iran's insistence that it must keep on enriching uranium and that the West had no business interfering. He made speeches calling for the destruction of the nation of Israel and the total defeat of the United States. Little progress was made toward repairing relations and talk of war between the West and Iran. Israel, which itself had secretly built nuclear weapons, declared its right to defend itself. Israel would, it said, bomb Iran's nuclear facilities if Iran were on the verge of building a weapon. Ahmadinejad repeated his call for Israel's destruction.

In June 2013, Hassan Fereydoon Rouhani, 64, was elected president of Iran, replacing Ahmadinejad. He criticized the direction Iran had been heading in the nuclear stand-off with the West. He pointed to the bad state of Iran's economy that had resulted due to trade sanctions, or limitations, that the United States and other Western nations had imposed as punishment for Iran's continuation of uranium processing. Iran had been largely isolated from the rest of the world, and that was hurting the country. Rouhani immediately started negotiations which, in 2013, led to an interim treaty with the West on Iran's nuclear program.

Iranians hold posters of President Hassan Rouhani to show their support in 2013.

INTERNET LINKS

www.ancient.eu.com/Persia
The Ancient History Encyclopedia has a good overview with many good articles, images, and maps.

www.iranchamber.com
The Iran Chamber Society offers excellent articles on Iranian history, arts, and culture.

www.factmonster.com/ipka/A0107640.html
Fact Monster provides a good overview of Iran's recent history.

GOVERNMENT

The flag of Iran flutters against the brilliant blue sky.

3

O N PAPER, IRAN'S 1979 CONSTITUTION looks like that of a modern democracy. It guarantees a number of freedoms and a way for Iranians to vote for an assembly and a president. But there are crucial differences.

A UNIQUE GOVERNMENT

Iran is governed based on the constitution that was approved in a national referendum following the revolution in 1979. A national referendum in 1989 approved amendments to the constitution of 1979.

Iran's constitution is unique. It is based on a new concept—Islamic government—created by Ayatollah Khomeini. This system of government rules according to God's law first, and then the law of men.

The supreme leader, the *vali-ye faqih* (VAH-li-yee fah-kee), is elected for life by an Assembly of Experts—a committee of eighty-six theologians who are publicly elected to an eight-year term. The faqih is respected for his theological knowledge and has final authority in all decisions made by the executive, legislative, and judicial branches. The faqih can veto any legislation passed by the executive branch. The current faqih is Ayatollah Seyed Ali Khamenei.

THE PRESIDENT

The executive branch of the Iranian government consists of a Council of Ministers headed by a president. Before 1989 the executive branch included a prime minister, who chose the members of the cabinet and

Since the 1979 revolution, the Islamic penal code in Iran includes punishments such as stoning, floggings, and amputations. The age at which offenders are held responsible as adults for criminal activity is nine for girls and fifteen for boys.

led executive duties, and the president, who filled a largely ceremonial position. Constitutional amendments in 1989 removed the prime minister and expanded the role of the president. The president is now the head of government and is elected to a four-year term. In 2013, Iranians elected Hassan Rouhani to be the president.

LAWS AND COURTS

An Islamic Consultative Assembly called the *Majlis* (MAHJ-lis) drafts legislation. The 290 members of the Majlis are publicly elected for four-year terms. A Council of Guardians reviews any legislation passed by the Majlis to ensure that it follows *Sharia*, or Islamic law. The council is made up of twelve jurists—six are chosen by the faqih, and six are recommended by the head of the judiciary and then appointed by the Majlis.

Iranian President Hassan Rouhani at a meeting in Tehran in 2014

The Council of Guardians has the power to strike down and send back to the Majlis for revision any legislation it deems not in line with Islamic law or the constitution. When disputes arise between the Majlis and the Council of Guardians, the Expediency Council mediates. This council includes some of Iran's most powerful men, who are appointed by the faqih. The council's chairman is Ayatollah Ahmad Jannati.

The judicial branch of the Iranian government consists of the Supreme Court and a network of subordinate courts. Besides civil and criminal courts, there are special courts in Iran that hear charges of clerical misconduct or terrorism and national security offenses.

Iranian forces stand for review for President Khatami.

LOCAL GOVERNMENT

At the local level, Iran is divided into twenty-eight provinces, each divided into counties, and each county has several districts and subdistricts. The Ministry of the Interior appoints a governor to each province and each county, and a mayor to each city.

DEFENSE

The commander-in-chief of Iran's armed forces is not the president, but the faqih. The faqih decides on all matters concerning national security and defense. The Supreme National Security Council organizes internal and external defense. The council includes the president, leaders of the armed forces and the Revolutionary Guard, and ministers in charge of foreign and internal affairs.

Iran's armed forces consist of the army and the Revolutionary Guard. The army protects the nation's territory against foreign intrusion or invasion;

the Revolutionary Guard enforces Islamic law in daily life and monitors opponents to the regime. The Revolutionary Guard has also supported Islamic revolutionary movements in other countries.

ELECTIONS

Iran holds presidential and parliamentary elections every four years. Political parties include the Islamic Iran Participation Front (the largest reformist party), the conservative Followers of the Imam's Line, and the Green Party, which campaigns for the natural environment and against the production of nuclear, chemical, and biological weapons.

Election candidates have to be Muslim Iranian citizens age twenty-five and over, and they must be loyal to the faqih. Election committees screen all applicants, but the Council of Guardians makes the final approval or

Iranians cast votes in the presidential election in 2013.

rejection. Candidates can start campaigning only after the final list of approved applicants has been issued.

Iranians are eligible to vote for government leaders from age fifteen. Women and youth are a growing voice in the electorate.

POWER STRUGGLE

Deep rifts in the government are the main reason for Iran's slow, problematic reforms. Two camps are caught in a power struggle—the reformists led by President Rouhani and the conservatives led by Ayatollah Khamenei.

The reformists are pushing for a more democratic Iran while the conservatives are clinging to the strict codes of the revolution. These strong differences in opinion continue to hinder social, economic, and political reforms that would improve the country's global image.

Grand Ayatollah Ali Khamenei, the current Supreme Leader of Iran

سال حماسه سیاسی، حماسه اقتصادی

رینگ ها | کاربر محیر | خدمات اپراتنی | خبرو آموزشی | خانواده و سرگرمی | خبری | فرهنگی و مذهبی

ولادت حضرت فاطمه زهرا سلام الله علیها، روز مادر و روز زن مبارک باد

CENSORSHIP

For conservatives, the role of the mass media is to propagate Islamic culture and avoid supporting anti-Islamic culture. Publications have to be licensed, and the constitution guarantees press freedom. However, publications have been shut down and journalists jailed for printing articles deemed detrimental to Islam or the revolution.

Many newspapers have been banned or suspended, including *Nourooz*, an Iranian daily newspaper, which moved onto the Internet, and the similarly named *Ruz-e Now*. Many pro-reformist journalists have been tried in the revolutionary courts and sentenced to serve jail terms.

In the early 2000s, many banned publications used the Internet as an alternate route to reaching audiences. At that time, media censorship in Iran had not caught up with media technology, and thousands of Iranians with access to the Internet were able to read publications that the government was trying to silence. However, the authorities eventually cracked down and now, in the second decade of the twenty-first century, Iran has an extensive list of banned sites that have been blocked.

Radio, TV, film, and even museum and gallery exhibits are subject to censorship. Most forms of media are reviewed for acceptability by the Ministry of Culture and Islamic guidance. The international journalists' organization Reporters Without Borders ranks Iran's press situation as "very serious"—the worst ranking on its five-point scale.

When Iranians try to access Facebook, they see this page instead, with text praising the president. Social media is blocked in Iran.

POLITICAL FIGURES

Several politicians and religious leaders have been central to the emergence and development of the Islamic Republic of Iran. In particular, Ayatollah Khomeini was the first vali-ye faqih. Indeed, the revolution that brought about the fall of the monarchy was called in his name.

Born in 1900, Khomeini was trained as a clergyman and in the 1930s became one of the leaders in the opposition to Reza Shah. In 1964 Khomeini was exiled from Iran and fled to Iraq. In 1978 he fled to France. While in exile, he organized the opposition to the shah that in 1979 led to the successful overthrow of the monarchy.

Khomeini was able to bring about his vision of a new Islamic order, free from Western influence. He succeeded because of his charisma and because many of his contemporaries shared his anti-Americanism, which was vividly expressed in posters and slogans during the revolution. Despite misgivings among some of the clergy, Khomeini's plan to turn Iran into a strictly religious society was put in place. Khomeini became the unquestioned leader of Iran and stayed in power unchallenged until his death in 1989.

INTERNET LINKS

www.president.ir
The official website of the president of Iran. Choose English.

www.aljazeera.com/indepth/features/2014/01/iran-1979-revolution-shook-world-2014121134227652609.html
"Iran 1979: The Revolution that Shook the World"
An excellent analysis written in 2014.

tehrantimes.com/politics
Tehran Times: Politics and world news from an Iranian point of view.

ECONOMY

Pistachios are one of Iran's most important crops.

4

THE MOST IMPORTANT WORD THAT describes Iran's economy has only three letters: o-i-l. Iran, in fact, sits on a sea of oil and natural gas. Underneath the country's plains and mountains lie an estimated 125.8 billion barrels of crude oil, one-tenth of the world's entire known reserves. However, the role of oil in Iran's economy is declining, perhaps as a reaction to the trade sanctions imposed by the West in 2003 in response to Iran's secretive nuclear program. The sanctions were meant to pressure Iran to cooperate with the West, but might instead have forced the country to diversify its economy, and expand beyond its reliance on oil as its main export.

Iran's economy expanded at a very fast pace in the second half of the twentieth century. During this time the government built gigantic steel plants, oil refineries, and factories.

The Iran-Iraq war, which lasted through most of the 1980s, disrupted economic development in Iran. The war resulted in more than a million deaths in Iran and extensive damage to the country's natural environment and economic infrastructure. Iran's production of crude oil, an important revenue source, dipped drastically after bombing raids damaged oil fields.

Signs of recovery began to show after the war. In 2003 Iran's crude-oil-production capacity surpassed 2.2 million barrels per day. Because of the economic sanctions imposed by Western nations that year, however, Iran's oil exports had sunk to a low of 700,000 barrels per day by May 2013.

Iran is largely self-sufficient in food production for domestic consumption. Large-scale irrigation projects have made desert areas agriculturally productive and have significantly expanded the country's agricultural output.

AGRICULTURE

Agriculture accounts for 10 percent of Iran's gross domestic product and employs about 17 percent of the labor force. Only around 10 percent of Iran's land is arable, or able to be farmed. Most of the country's crops,

A pistachio tree in Bahreman village in southeastern Iran, where pistachio plantations extend for miles.

including sugar beets, cotton, and wool, are cultivated near the Caspian Sea, north of Tehran. Grains, especially wheat and rice, are the most important crops. Pistachio nuts are another big earner, as Iran produces 50 percent of the world's pistachios, making it the world's largest producer. Pistachios are Iran's third-largest export, after oil and carpets.

Livestock—sheep, goats, cattle, donkeys, horses, and camels—are used for their services in transportation and in plowing fields, or for their hide or milk to make food and other products.

Access to the Caspian Sea and the Persian Gulf has led to the growth of an active fishing industry, particularly in caviar—sturgeon eggs.

HEAVY INDUSTRY

The Iranian economy depends heavily on the export of crude oil and natural gas, which account for more than 80 percent of export earnings. Iran's oil fields are located mainly in the southwestern province of Khuzestan and in the Persian Gulf. The country also claims some of the reserves in the Caspian Sea. Most of Iran's gas reserves lie in the Persian Gulf, in the South Pars field, shared with the tiny country of Qatar. Oil and natural gas are transported through pipelines both domestically and into neighboring countries. One such pipeline runs for about 1,590 miles (2,559 km) from Tabriz in the north to Ankara in Turkey.

Iran's non-oil industries have been growing since the 1990s, as the government places increasing emphasis on reducing the country's dependence on oil and gas revenues. Iran's non-oil industries include, apart from agriculture, the extraction of minerals and metals and the manufacture of industrial goods such as automobiles and tractors. Most of these industries are located in Tehran province.

Iranian police officers patrol part of the Caspian Sea in front of an oil facility.

PERSIAN CARPETS

The artistry of Persian carpets inspired the imaginary flying carpet, or magic carpet, many centuries ago. The motif shows up in folktales and other stories to this day.

One of Iran's most famous crafts is also one of its oldest. Persian carpets are legendary. Indeed, the magic carpet, or flying carpet, has its origins in Middle Eastern folktales. It's easy to see how the beauty of these carpets could inspire magic.

Persian carpets are also legendary for their intricate patterns, richness of color, and fine quality. Persian carpet weaving has a very long history. For centuries, Persian rugs have been at the center of the home. People kneel on carpets to pray and sit to eat. Nomads placed carpets at the entrance to their tents and covered the ground inside the tent so that they could sit or sleep more comfortably. The oldest rug believed to be of Persian origin dates back to around 500 BCE. It was discovered in 1949 in the Siberian Altai region.

Authentic Persian carpets are handmade from natural fibers and are valued internationally for their beauty and quality, the result of a deep-

Carpet weaving is a specialized, laborious, and time-consuming art. It may take as long as a year or two to finish one carpet by the traditional method of a knotted stitch, done on a loom. There are mainly two kinds of knotted stitch: a Turkish knot, which involves the use of a needle; and a Persian knot, which is made without a needle and used for very fine carpets. One square yard of high-quality carpet may have up to a million knots, and an average carpet about 200,000. Usually, a highly-skilled weaver can make about 12,000 knots a day.

When the weaving is finished, the carpet has to go through two more processes: the fibers are crushed to make the carpet pliable; and then the carpet is washed and dried. In some areas, such as the Rey neighborhood near Tehran, these processes have become a tourist attraction.

rooted artisan tradition. There are many carpet-producing regions in Iran; two of the more famous Persian weaves come from the Hamadan region and Bijar in Kermanshah province. Iran exports most of its carpets to Europe, especially Germany.

HANDICRAFT PRODUCTION

Apart from its world-renowned carpets, Iran has several other handicraft traditions. Hamadan is known for its pottery, ceramics, and leather works. From Gorgan and Mashhad come bonnets, embroidered sheepskin coats, and dresses, tunics, and blouses made from natural silk, known as *kalaghe* (KAH-lah-gi). Bakhtaran, the largest city in western Iran, produces knitted footwear.

The Khorasan mine in Mashhad produces turquoise, which is worked

Bazaars are an important institution in Iran that date back thousands of years. These marketplaces range from tented street fairs to huge indoor mall-like spaces. All are important places for the selling and buying of goods. But they are more than that. Although there are air-conditioned shopping centers in the cities, bazaars are gathering places where news is discussed, social connections are made, and political intrigue may hatch. The colorful marketplaces offer a wide array of consumer products, but may also be the places to find smuggled illegal goods.

Throughout history, bazaar merchants played a crucial role in local economies, and therefore had a good deal of influence over politics and policies.

The bazaars in the present capital city Tehran and in a former capital city Isfahan are particularly famous and picturesque. The Tehran Grand Bazaar, *with two hundred thousand vendors, covering nearly 8 square miles (20 sq. km.), and with up to two million visitors a day, is the largest market of its type on Earth.*

into all kinds of jewelry. Timber is rare in Iran, and therefore woodwork and wooden items are not high on the crafts list, but wooden carvings and wooden kitchen tools are sold around the Caucasus mountains and near the Caspian Sea. Pottery, ceramics, and glasswork, however, can be found throughout Iran. Pottery, especially, has experienced a recent revival and renaissance led by the National Crafts School in Tehran.

TOURISM

Iran has many assets that make it an excellent tourist destination. The country's diverse terrain offers visitors the chance to ski in the mountains or sunbathe on the beaches of the Persian Gulf or the Caspian Sea. In addition, the land itself is exceptionally picturesque. Many travelers visit Iran for its architecture, its historical and archaeological sites, and its handicraft bazaars and museum exhibitions.

Although Iran's conservative leaders worry about the cultural influence of foreign tourists on the citizens of the country, the official stand on tourism remains one of welcome. Iran aims to take advantage of the economic potential of its tourism industry by developing tourist facilities, such as information centers, as well as training guides and translators.

Most tourists to Iran come from neighboring countries such as Saudi Arabia and Azerbaijan, while Germans make up the largest number of Western tourists. The number of tourist arrivals from the West fell after the September 11, 2001, terrorist attacks in the United States, but that trend has been reversing. In 2011, the number of foreign tourists in Iran reached 3 million visitors, who brought more than $2 billion to the country's economy.

INTERNET LINKS

www.tehrantimes.com/economy-and-business
The *Tehran Times* is Iran's English-language newspaper.

www.state.gov/e/eb/tfs/spi/iran/index.htm
The U.S. State Department page regarding trade sanctions against Iran.

www.npr.org/blogs/parallels/2014/03/15/290237837/economic-sanctions-play-out-in-strange-ways-in-iran
NPR audio and transcript of a report about the effects of trade sanctions against Iran.

www.bbc.com/news/world-middle-east-15983302
BBC: "Q&A: Iran Sanctions" explains the sanctions in a question-and-answer format.

ENVIRONMENT

Air pollution causes smog in Tehran, particularly in the winter months.

5

RAN HAS LONG BEEN KNOWN FOR its clear water and healthful air, especially in the mountains. But industrial development, the proliferation of automobiles and trucks, and the development of the oil industry have created a pollution problem in some parts of the country.

Iran sits on a high plateau, surrounded by mountains, with the Persian Gulf to the south and the Caspian Sea to the north. Archaeologists believe that nomads have been living in the region for nearly 100,000 years. Perhaps around 7000 BCE, some nomads settled down with their herds of animals and began farming crops.

In a land where the climate was hot and water scarce, these small populations managed to survive. In the last century, however, high population growth, rapid urban expansion, and the demands of a modernizing economy have posed serious challenges to Iran's natural environment—challenges that persist and that threaten to worsen, unless strong measures are taken, in the twenty-first century.

AIR POLLUTION

Air pollution is a serious health problem in the capital and other major cities. The main source of pollutants is traffic. Nearly a quarter of the cars in Tehran are more than twenty years old. These cars have poor exhaust systems and use low-grade leaded fuel. Sometimes the air gets

The air quality in Tehran can become so dangerous that some people wear masks to go outside.

so bad in Tehran that schools have to close and people have to wear masks or stay indoors. Surrounded by mountains, the city gets trapped in smog. The pollution also affects mountain wildlife.

A yellowish blanket of smog regularly hangs over the capital city of Tehran around the same time every year, in the winter months. In January 2013, conditions in Tehran were so dangerous that officials ordered government offices, schools, universities, and banks to close for five days to help ease the pollution. Four of Iran's cities were on the list of the world's ten most polluted cities, as reported by the World Health Organization. In 2014, city health officials said some 270 people were dying each day from blood cancer, heart and respiratory diseases, and other pollution-related illnesses.

WATER POLLUTION

Pollution has also struck Iran's waters, which include the Persian Gulf, the Caspian Sea, and the country's lakes and rivers. The sources of water pollutants include farms, factories, offshore oil rigs, and coastal housing and tourist resorts. Most of the world's sturgeon live in the Caspian Sea, where they used to be in abundance. But water pollution and overfishing have reduced sturgeon populations so drastically that these fish are now in danger of extinction.

It is difficult to monitor and regulate the flow of pollutants into the Caspian Sea partly because it is bordered by several countries. Pollutants may enter the sea via, for example, Russia's Volga River or Azerbaijan's Kura River. Finding an effective solution to pollution in the Caspian Sea depends on the cooperation of all the countries involved.

The Persian Gulf is in a similar situation, being one of the major oil-producing regions in the world. Rigs in the gulf drill out 30,000 to 40,000 barrels of oil every day. Some of this oil escapes into the gulf through cracks in the rigs. In addition, waste water released into the gulf by oil companies is high in salt, which raises water temperatures, making it unbearable for fish living in the gulf.

DROUGHT

In August 2000 the Zayandeh Rud River dried up during one of the worst droughts in Iranian history. In fact, the drought continued for more than a decade. During that time, major lakes such as the great Bakhtegan shrank. Lake Urmia, once one of the largest salt lakes in the world, lost 95 percent of its water. The former tourist destination in the northwestern part of Iran literally withered away—not just the water, but the livelihoods of the people in the surrounding communities. Water in reservoirs around the country fell to very low levels. Iran suffered such severe water shortages that it needed international aid to pull through the devastating drought.

With very little rainfall, drought is a major environmental problem in Iran. Prolonged drought destroys the country's wetlands, the natural habitats of aquatic plants and animals and of birds living in these areas. Wildlife die from starvation and disease, and rural residents lose their means of livelihood as their crops and livestock die.

An abandoned boat is stuck in the solidified salts at Lake Urmia after the saltwater lake shrank to a fraction of its former size.

An old garden was destroyed to make room for new buildings.

To respond to these devastating droughts, Iran built huge dams to control the storage and distribution of water. But dam construction has brought about other environmental problems, such as creating breeding grounds for disease in stagnant water. Dams on rivers also hinder the movement of fresh water into the gulf, thus worsening the plight of the gulf's fish population. And dams are blamed for the desiccation of Lake Urmia.

In 2014, Iranian President Hassan Rouhani said water was a national security issue—indeed, demonstrations and riots over water supplies had already broken out.

THREAT TO BIODIVERSITY

The term *biodiversity*, or biological diversity, refers to the variety of plants and animals that live in a specific area. A major environmental challenge in many countries is protecting this natural diversity from the harmful activities of modern society. The danger is especially great for endemic plant and animal species, which are unique to a country or region and cannot be found in any other part of the world.

Deforestation takes place when trees are cleared to make space for housing, and to provide fuel or raw materials for construction and paper manufacture. Desertification, or the expansion of desert land, occurs where fields are overgrazed or where farmers use poor cultivation techniques. Deforestation and desertification have led to the extinction of several plants and animals in Iran.

As Iran's human population grows, more and more land is taken over for housing and farming—over 230 square miles (596 square km) of forests are cleared each year. Wild animals that lose their homes this way have to compete for food with domesticated animals, and they are often killed by farmers.

To protect Iran's natural environment, the government has embarked on reforestation programs and sand-dune stabilization efforts to control desertification. There are also laws aimed at protecting plants and animals and fighting pollution, such as the Environmental Protection and Enhancement Act.

PROTECTING THE ENVIRONMENT

Under Iran's constitution, protecting the environment is considered a public duty, and surveys have shown that Iranians care strongly about the environment. However, political instability due to a revolution and a war have hindered conservation efforts until recently. Conservation is now a major priority in government policy. National parks and wildlife refuges have been established, and fish-culture programs are helping to replenish dwindling sturgeon populations in the Caspian Sea.

Due to an increasing population and rapid modernization, energy consumption in Iran has tripled since 1980. This has been a major contributor to the country's pollution problem. The destructive effects of rising energy consumption on the natural environment are wide-ranging and long-lasting. Apart from producing more pollutants through the burning of fossil fuels, it places a heavy strain on Iran's enormous—yet limited fuel—resources. (The government is considering alternative forms of energy, such as solar, wind, and tidal power. Nuclear energy is also being explored, despite international opposition.) Another way oil and gas exploration has damaged the environment is through the use of massive machines to dig into the earth, sometimes under mountains.

Environmental groups such as the Green Party of Iran and the Green Front of Iran have to work within tremendous political and economic constraints because Iran is still adjusting politically and socially and has limited financial resources. The biggest challenge for the country is to balance economic development with environmental protection.

Among Iran's threatened animal species is the Baluchistan black bear, a subspecies of the Asiatic black bear native to the Himalaya Mountains. Asiatic black bears, close cousins of the American black bear, have larger ears and a V-shaped white patch on the chest. The Baluchistan black bear was once thought to be extinct, but was later rediscovered and is now considered critically endangered. It lives in forested areas near waterholes in the arid southern regions of Iran: Kerman, Hormozgan, and Baluchistan. Deforestation has greatly reduced the bears' natural habitat, and farmers kill them to protect their livestock and crops. In addition, recent drought has also taken a toll on the bear population and conservationists fear it will in fact go extinct without active intervention.

Baliuchistan black bear

The Caspian tiger, or Persian tiger, once lived in parts of the Middle East and Russia. Forest clearing near the Caspian Sea to make way for farming forced the tiger out of its natural habitat. Unable to adapt as well to other areas, the Caspian tiger gradually disappeared and is now believed to be extinct. None have been seen since the early 1970s, and there are none living in captivity anywhere in the world. The Iranian lion had the same fate. Originally living in the southern Zagros Mountains, the lion was hunted for sport by royalty, one of the main causes of the lion's extinction. Meanwhile, Iran's cheetah and leopard populations are dwindling, while jackals and hyenas are fighting for survival against human encroachment into their natural habitats.

Caspian tiger

Persian fallow deer once roamed a large part of the Middle East and northeastern Africa. They have been thought to be extinct a few times in the past, only to be rediscovered in a secluded location. In the 1950s, a small population was found in a forested area in western Iran, near the border with Iraq. Laws were put in place to conserve the remaining Persian fallow deer, but since the war with Iraq in the 1980s, it is not known for certain how many are left. It is classified as endangered and remains one of the world's rarest deer species.

There is hope for some of Iran's threatened species if prompt and proper action is taken to protect them. The yellow deer, for example, is no longer on the threatened species list (it has not gone into the extinct species list). After efforts by the government and by conservationists, the yellow deer population is growing.

Persian fallow deer

INTERNET LINKS

iranprimer.usip.org/blog/2013/oct/28/iran%E2%80%99s-environment-greater-threat-foreign-foes
Iran Primer: "Iran's Environment is a Greater Threat than Foreign Foes."

www.persianwildlife.us
The Persian Wildlife Foundation is a U.S. organization interested in conservation in Iran.

IRANIANS

An Iranian girl in Isfahan smiles.

6

WHO ARE THE IRANIAN PEOPLE? Unlike most Middle Eastern countries, Iran is not an Arab country, nor is Arabic the national language. Iran is Persian. However, while Persians make up most of Iran's population, there are significant non-Persian ethnic groups scattered about the country.

Iran has a population of more than 76.4 million people. Most Iranians live in the northern part of the country, where the capital is located. Central Iran, with its hills and deserts, is sparsely populated. Climate plays a role in population density and the way social life is structured in Iran. As in much of the Middle East, people from the harsh desert and semi-desert environments tend to live and group together differently than those from the lush, fertile coastal areas and valleys.

Iranians are known for their hospitality, which stems partly from the fragility of life in a harsh land, where people have to depend on one another for many of their basic needs.

TRIBES AND CLANS

Among nomads, the basic unit of a community is the tribe, usually ruled by a chieftain. There are also tribes that have settled in villages. However, nomads generally consider themselves superior to villagers, so they will always acknowledge their nomadic background and ancestry.

A nomadic campsite is made up of the tents of the families of the

Iran has by far the largest Jewish population of any Muslim country. In fact, Judaism in Persia dates back to biblical times. However, today's Jewish population is quite small, relative to the rest of Iran's minority ethnicities. Many demographic maps do not even list the Iranian Jews. Various estimates report the current Jewish population in Iran to be around 10,800–many thousands of Iranian Jews having emigrated after the 1979 revolution.

A group of Qashqai nomads set up camp in the province of Fars in southern Iran.

tribe. The tent protects the family from the desert winds and is surrounded by a fence to keep out wild animals. The tents and fences are collapsible and can be easily mounted on horses or camels whenever the tribe moves to greener pastures or to look for water at oases.

Within a nomadic tribe, there are elaborate customs dictating each person's behavior, lines of authority among members of the tribe, and marriage patterns between families. These customs are necessary to maintain strong family bonds and to preserve the tribal structure.

In the villages, the most important social groups are the clan and the family. A few interrelated families make up a clan. Each family may live in a mud-brick home in the village compound.

Many villages in Iran consist of just one clan, while larger villages may have several clans. Within the clan, one's family comes first. Loyalty to the family is important in the villager's daily life and even for his or her survival.

Families in a clan usually work together and mingle in their daily social activities. They share whatever good fortune or bad luck comes their way. Thus village communities tend to be tight-knit and united, with a strong sense of belonging to the clan.

URBANIZATION AND TRADITION

In Iran's cities, the tribe and clan have lost almost all of the significance they have in nomadic and village communities. In the cities, the role of tribe and clan is taken over by the extended family—a network of blood relations that includes grandparents, aunts, uncles, and cousins. Although urban Iranian families may not always live together under one roof, they do take one another's concerns very seriously.

The average Iranian family is getting smaller, in some part, as living standards rise. While the average number of children per family in Iran—about six—is still very high when compared to families in the Western world, the figure is still lower than that in most other Middle Eastern countries.

Despite growing Western influences, especially in the cities, Iranians have maintained their traditional strong sense of family. They visit one another, spend quality time together, and talk over family dinners. Religious values

The Alborz Mountains rise up just north of Tehran.

and customs persist, especially in rural areas. In a traditional Muslim family, divisions exist by gender. For instance, there are areas of the house just for family and areas where unrelated male guests are entertained by male family members.

The practice of polygamy—Islamic law allows a man to take four wives—is gradually declining. While a man can divorce his wife anytime, a woman needs her husband's written permission to file for divorce. However, women's divorce rights in Iran are being reviewed.

ETHNIC GROUPS

Iran is a multiethnic society of mainly Persians, Azeri, Kurds, Arabs, Baluchis, Lur, and Turks. Nomadic minorities and foreigners constitute a very small percentage of the population. The largest ethnic groups are the Persians, who make up half of the population, and the Azeri, who account for 16 percent of Iranians.

PERSIANS The Persians have their origins in an ancient culture. They are an Indo-European people, whose ancestors are believed to have come from Central Asia around 2000 BCE From around 550 BCE Persia became a powerful empire and ruled vast territories as far away as India.

Persians today are proud of their history, immortalized in monuments from the various periods of Persian rule and still seen throughout the country, especially in Persepolis and Isfahan. When Iran's original name, Persia, was replaced in 1935, it signified the nation's transition into a new era of modernity, but also acknowledged its Persian roots, for *Iran* was derived from the ancient Persian language.

One attribute that identifies the Persians with other peoples of the Middle East is their shared religion, Islam. Yet the Persians have their own ethnic profile and culture, distinct from that of Arab and other Middle Eastern cultures.

AZERI AND KURDS Together the Azeri and the Kurds account for 26 percent of the Iranian population. These groups predominate in

northwestern Iran. They have made several bids for autonomy and supported the revolution, hoping that the removal of the shah would improve their position in Iranian society—but it did not. Khomeini continued the shah's trend to invest ultimate authority in the government, with one difference: he abolished democratic representation of various groups and peoples.

There are also Kurds in Iraq and Turkey. No matter where they live—whether as nomads or urbanites, they have managed to look after their own communities and to maintain their own language and religion.

ARABS Iran has a number of Arab people, although they are still a small minority, making up only 2 percent or so of the population. Arab-Iranians are concentrated in the southern province of Khuzestan. In fact, there are so many Arabs living here that some neighboring Arabic-speaking nations do not regard this region as being part of Iran. The Iraqis, for instance, still refer to the area as Arabestan, its name before Iran occupied it in the 1920s, and the province was a major point of contention in the Iran-Iraq war. Khuzestan

An Iranian Azeri man walks to his house in the cave village of Kandovan. There, people have built dwellings in the strange rock formations for some 3,000 years.

is important to Iran because it is rich in oil deposits.

Ethnic conflict has flared up occasionally, such as during the 1979 revolution. The Arabs demanded local autonomy, a greater share of the oil revenue, and an end to discrimination. Arabs in Iran feel that they are not getting a fair share of income or employment or a voice in politics.

NOMADS

Some estimates put the size of Iran's nomadic and semi-nomadic population at 3 to 4 percent of the total population, while others put it as high as 13 percent.

This variation is partly due to different definitions of nomads: some move freely their entire lives; others follow a set path and area; yet others have established homesteads in a few locations.

Most nomads are organized in tribes, such as the Bakhtiari, Baluchi, Lur, and Khamseh. Politically, the role of nomads has not been an easy one. Every Iranian ruler has tried to harness nomadic tribes and settle them in fixed locations. This effort has in recent decades achieved only partial success. The nomads remain largely self-sufficient: their herds provide them with food and milk, hair or wool to spin yarn and weave clothes and carpets, and hides to make tent covers.

The proverb "where thy carpet lies is thy house" has true meaning in nomadic life. Many nomads get by without using money. The few goods they want, they barter for in town markets in exchange for their rugs or milk.

A Qashqai woman holds spinning wool in Fars province.

QASHQAI Over the last two centuries, one nomadic group in particular has acquired some political significance. These are the Qashqai, who live in the area around Shiraz and who have their own confederacy. During the early years of the modern state of Iran, the existence of subgroups such as the Qashqai, with their own laws, leaders, and independence, was seen as a threat.

In 1979 several leaders of the Qashqai, called khans, returned from exile once they knew that the shah had been overthrown. They generally commanded authority among their own people, and some of them became very popular and charismatic leaders in the revolution. Initially they supported Khomeini, who was not quite as generous, having regarded the Qashqai as feudal barons and highway robbers.

Once the revolution was won, Khomeini crushed the political power of the Qashqai. In 1982 small groups of Qashqai in the mountains of southwestern Iran continued to defend themselves against Khomeini's Revolutionary Guard.

INTERNET LINKS

ngm.nationalgeographic.com/2008/08/iran-archaeology/del-giudice-text
National Geographic: "Persia: Ancient Soul of Iran"
Excellent article with photo gallery explores how the country's deep history informs the modern Iranian character.

www.theatlantic.com/international/archive/2012/06/the-iran-we-dont-see-a-tour-of-the-country-where-people-love-americans/258166/
The Atlantic: "The Iran We Don't See: A Tour of the Country Where People Love Americans"
A very human, alternative view of Iranian people.

LIFESTYLE

An Iranian schoolgirl heads home from school in Tehran.

7

LIFESTYLES IN IRAN VARY GREATLY. In the modern capital of Tehran, people live pretty much as they do in all the world's modern cities. In the countryside, the way of life very much depends on ancient traditions that are still valued today.

In Tehran, people are generally up and about by 7 a.m., ready for the hustle and bustle of a work day in the city. Shops on the streets open for business, selling newspapers and hot beverages. Factories start at 7 or 7:30 a.m., while government offices open at 8 a.m. and banks at 8:30 a.m. The average work day for employees in commercial offices is usually eight hours long, while small business owners typically work ten hours a day. School starts at 8 a.m.

A common work practice in Iran is an extended lunch break, usually two hours long, whether in government offices, factories, or schools and universities. In the summer months, the lunch break may be even longer, but people work later into the evening.

Some workers lunch at restaurants and then take a nap in a park or at home. Most go home to have lunch with their family. This way, family members get to see one another not just in the evening but in the day as well. The self-employed also have an extended lunch break, often four hours long in the middle of the day, as shops tend to stay open until 10 p.m. so that their customers can shop after work.

Friday is the day of prayer, so government offices, banks, and schools close from Thursday afternoon through the whole of Friday. The self-employed also close their shops for at least half the day to take a break from their businesses and go to the mosque.

In Iran, dogs are not man's best friend. Owning a pet dog is frowned upon, and some officials have tried to ban dog ownership altogether. Many Iranians consider dogs to be unclean. Officials say pets pose "a cultural problem" that is the "blind imitation of the vulgar Western culture." They warn that dog ownership leads to family corruption and damages societal values. In Tehran, police have been arresting people for walking dogs in public or for having dogs in their cars.

A high-school student takes a university entrance exam.

EDUCATION

In the 1960s the Iranian government undertook large-scale reforms to improve public education. Many schools, teacher-training institutes, and universities were built during this period. Student enrollment in public schools increased, the quality of education improved, and literacy levels rose. In the 1970s universities in the major cities were expanded.

However, developments in the education system benefited people in the cities more than it did villagers, resulting in an urban-rural literacy disparity. There is also a male-female disparity, with a higher literacy rate for men than for women. Apart from the traditional view that women do not need formal education, women also face legislative barriers to entry into foreign universities.

Elementary school is compulsory for children ages six to twelve, but some children do not attend, either because the school is too far away or they have to work in the family business or on the family farm. High school is not compulsory and is generally free of charge. Every high-school year finishes with major examinations. Should a student fail a subject (out of as many as twelve), he or she has to repeat the entire year.

The school week starts on Saturday morning at 8 a.m. and finishes on Thursday at lunchtime. The school year begins in September and, except for a two-week holiday in March for the Islamic New Year, carries on until June the following year without a break. About 95 percent of Iranian children are enrolled in schools, most in public schools. In recent years, private schools have sprung up to cater to the wealthy. Getting a place in one of the state universities is not easy; more than a million students attend private universities. Many wealthy Iranians send their children to study in Europe and even as far away as Australia.

Lacking adequate facilities and resources, Iran's education sector is ill-equipped to handle the demand from a large, young population and has far to go in trying to catch up with education in many other countries.

CITY LIFE

Iran has grown increasingly urban since the middle of the twentieth century. By 1988 more than half the total population was living in urban areas, which experienced an annual growth rate twice that in rural areas. By the same year, around 18 million people were living in forty cities with populations of more than 100,000. By 2000, cities such as Isfahan, Tabriz, and Shiraz had populations of at least 1 million. Population expansion has been fastest in Tehran, the capital, where some 10 million people live, making it Iran's most populous city.

Despite having large populations, Iran's big cities manage to keep open spaces and elegant avenues lined with trees. Rows of small specialized shops border the pavements. There are also multilevel supermarket complexes in the bigger cities. Iranian cities can generally be classified as traditional or modern cities.

TRADITIONAL CITIES The traditional city is easily recognized by three features. First, there is a mosque in the center, usually at the intersection

Mashhad, in northeast Iran, is the second-most populous city in the country.

of two major roads. This mosque is not just a place for prayer; with its large courtyard, it also serves as a meeting place for groups of people. Second, near the mosque are the city government buildings or the palace where a ruler used to live. Third, small streets branch out in all directions from the city center, with at least one serving as the main bazaar area of the city.

The traditional city is structured with its center as a hub of faith, power, and trade. Streets tend to be very congested with people on their way to the mosque and to the markets, where livestock, produce, and other goods are sold and bought.

In Iran, bazaars are more than places of trade; they have a distinct cultural and historical significance. Iran's bazaars continue to function much as they have for centuries. They have been studied by architects as models of organized structure and design. Each bazaar is arranged in a logical layout, with rows and alleys that separate stores selling specific items. Products such as carpets, fabrics, jewelry, pottery, or spices are displayed in different sections within the bazaar complex. Bazaar life stimulates the senses with food smells, the sounds of buyers bargaining, the colors of traditional handicrafts, and the nonstop movement of people and animals.

MODERN CITIES In the modern city, much of the raw, intimate atmosphere of the traditional city is gone. One of the main differences, compared to the traditional city, is that the modern city is not people-centered; instead, it is car-centered. In Tehran, boulevards are often eight lanes wide. In the business center, with its administrative buildings, are hotels, cinemas, restaurants, and department stores.

TRAFFIC Despite having wide streets, Iran's larger cities still suffer from traffic congestion and its consequent dangers. Driving in Tehran can be a nightmare—drivers do not always stop at traffic lights and rarely give signals to let others know what they intend to do. The resulting frenzy, made very audible by the constant honking of horns, often causes traffic jams that can take hours to unravel.

To deal with road problems in the capital, the Tehran Traffic Control Company was set up in 1991. It uses a traffic management system based on a

modern communications network to monitor and control the flow of traffic and reduce the occurrence of accidents. The city is also trying to improve its highway system. In 2007, there were 87 miles (130 km) of highways and 75 miles (120 km) of ramps and loops under construction. Another way to ease the traffic problem is to encourage people to take the bus or train to work instead of driving their own cars.

This view of western Tehran shows neighborhoods of low-rise housing.

Driving in the countryside is far easier, though buses and herds of animals may slow the pace. Gravel roads are generally rutted, and the distances between gasoline stations are long—62 miles (100 km) or more apart. There are also paved highways in the countryside, which makes travel a little faster.

HOUSING Urban housing by necessity tends to be more compact and carefully planned than rural housing. The type and style of housing and materials used in construction also differ.

Living costs can be extremely high in Iran's large cities. In Tehran, for example, professionals may spend as much as half their salaries on their housing rents, leaving very little for other expenses. Essentially, Iran's urban housing situation is no different than that in many other countries. City people tend to be neither very rich nor very poor, and they live in relatively modest accommodation. The problem of overcrowding in Iranian cities is made worse by the large size of many families.

RURAL LIFE

Despite the gradual migration of Iranians to the cities, there are still thousands of small villages scattered around the country. These isolated communities have managed to preserve many of their traditional customs and to sustain their old way of life amid technological change in the modernized parts of the country.

In the countryside, life's rhythm is dictated by the seasons and the time of day. Small villages, especially those in inaccessible areas, have no electricity, heating, or piped water. Human activity, like much of nature's activity, follows

An elderly shepherd leads a donkey.

the sun, starting as it rises and ending as it sets. Oil lamps provide some—but not enough—light in the evening for villagers to spin yarn or weave carpets. Similarly, most of the other regular chores have to be completed during the day: clothes have to be washed and dried, food has to be cooked, water has to be carried from the village well, the fields have to be tended and the animals fed, and so on.

While many villages still depend on manual and animal labor, others have started to experience a little luxury as machines such as tractors are gradually introduced to rural Iran.

VILLAGE LIFE In the villages, the problem of housing doesn't usually arise because many families own property. Largely because of a limited supply of timber or other building materials, and partly due to the hot climate, houses in the villages are usually made of mud bricks. Ninety percent of all village constructions in Iran are made of mud bricks. Mud bricks are often regarded as building material for the poor, being cheap and readily available. Mud bricks

Houses in the village of Laaft, on Qeshm Island in the Persian Gulf, have wind towers that channel cooling breezes into the home.

Iranian boys play in a water canal in one of Tehran's low-income neighborhoods.

are also useful because mud helps to keep the house cool in summer and warm in winter.

In addition, houses in desert or semi-desert areas usually have wind towers that trap wind and circulate the air to cool the house. The downside is that mud-brick houses cannot withstand earthquakes—they collapse easily.

Partly because of sandstorms, villagers usually build their homes close together. A large clay wall surrounds the village, and inside is a maze of small lanes leading to the various homes. The wall has several purposes: it helps the villagers defend themselves against bandits and shields them from the elements—sandstorms, the cutting cold winter winds, and the strong winds of Central Asia that can blow at 124 miles per hour (200 km per hour) and last more than 100 days. Villages near the Caspian Sea do not have this high wall, as the plentiful vegetation there prevents winds from gaining such speed and destructive force.

There is no running water and no electricity in many of these villages. There is often only one real street in the village, which has a water channel, or *djuba* (ZHOO-bah), built in the middle. This is the main water supply and the lifeline of the entire village. The position of the djuba makes it difficult for an outsider to steal any of the village's water without being seen. Each family in the village enjoys privacy in their small enclosed courtyards. Inside a house, there is little furniture. Rugs are placed on the clay floor or hung as wall hangings.

Many villages in Iran accommodate just one clan of around thirty to fifty inhabitants. The harsh conditions of the desert—poor soil, too little water— make it difficult to support a larger community. Farming in the Iranian countryside is very hard work, and many villagers live at subsistence levels.

With its mountain villages, coastal villages, and desert villages, the Iranian countryside exhibits an interesting and beautiful array of architectural styles that demonstrate how well people have adapted to their natural environment.

LIFE EXPECTANCY

Life expectancy in Iran has improved dramatically in recent years. It currently stands at seventy years, only slightly lower than Western life-expectancy figures. There is, however, a high infant mortality rate. A rate of some forty deaths per 1,000 live births ranks quite high when compared to some less developed nations. (The infant mortality rate is the number of infant deaths before the age of one year per thousand live births in the total population. The rate is used to evaluate a country's overall health. For the sake of comparison, the rate in the United States is about six deaths per 1,000; and in Afghanistan, about 122 deaths per 1,000 live births, the worst infant mortality rate on Earth.)

Iranians do not receive pensions, and there is no social security for the aged. Care for the old is entirely in the hands of the family. As families are large and people spend a lot of time with their families even in the cities, it is natural for Iranians to look after their aging parents. They do not perceive this as a burden, but as a responsibility and a way to show gratitude.

The aged are traditionally highly respected. They are seen as holding the keys to wisdom and to family stability, and it is therefore regarded as proper and beneficial for Iranians to live with and care for their aging relatives.

INTERNET LINKS

www.al-monitor.com/pulse/iran-pulse
Al Monitor offers up-to-minute news and lifestyle features about Iran and other Middle Eastern countries.

www.pbs.org/wgbh/pages/frontline/tehranbureau/2012/12/ dispatch-a-faith-of-their-own-islam-and-iranian-youth.html
Tehran Bureau Dispatch: "A Faith of their Own"
Young Iranians share their views of Islam and the role it plays in their lives.

RELIGION

The Takyeh Amir Chakhmagh Complex Mosque in Yazd is considered one of the finest set of historic buildings in Iran. The structures date to the 15th century.

8

RELIGION IN MODERN-DAY IRAN IS all encompassing. Iran is a theocracy, a nation ruled by religious figures. Of course, that religion is Islam.

Islam is the fastest-growing religion in the world, with approximately 1.6 billion Muslims, or 23 percent of the world's population. Islam is second only to Christianity in its number of adherents.

Nearly all Iranians are Muslims; 89 percent of the total population belong to the Shia group, and 10 percent belong to the Sunni group. Zoroastrians, Christians, Jews, and Baha'i worshippers make up 1 percent of the population.

Muslims pray at the Nasir al-Molk Mosque in Shiraz.

Islam is most closely associated with the countries of the Middle East and North Africa. However, nearly two-thirds (62 percent) of the world's Muslims live in the Asia-Pacific region. In fact, more Muslims live in India and Pakistan (344 million combined) than in the entire Middle East-North Africa region (317 million). The country with the largest number (about 209 million) is Indonesia, where 87 percent of the population is Muslim.

Through its long history in Iran, Islam has molded Iranian culture and influenced people's values, attitudes, and behaviors. More than that, Iran is a religious state. That means that religious rules (in this case, Islamic rules) are synonymous with state rules. The teachings of Islam, as interpreted by Khomeini and his followers, determine state life. Islam influences every aspect of people's lives, such as marriage laws, food practices, work hours, and school uniforms.

A clergyman holds up a Qur'an during a public demonstration demanding the world treat the Qur'an with respect.

LAWS OF ISLAM

Muslims believe that there is only one God. According to the Qur'an, the basic source of Islamic teaching, God is all-powerful, the creator of everything. Muslims believe that everyone will face a day of judgment, when God will decide if they have led good or bad lives on earth and accordingly send them to heaven or hell.

The Qur'an emphasizes the social dimension of service to God. It sets forth general ethical and legal principles to guide all aspects of Islamic living. The Qur'an does not constitute a comprehensive code of laws, but it does include rules on a broad variety of matters, including modesty, marriage, divorce, adultery, fornication, inheritance, intoxicants, diet, gambling, feuding, theft, and murder.

The Qur'an is not the only source of Islamic law. The *Sunnah* (SOON-nah) forms the other indispensable guide to the Islamic faith and legal system. It includes all the known sayings of the Prophet Muhammad, his decisions, and his responses to life situations and to philosophical and legal questions.

Six collections of Sunnah written in the ninth and tenth centuries are accepted as authoritative by most Muslims. Analogical reasoning and community consensus are the other official sources of Islamic law recognized in classical Islamic jurisprudence. Over the centuries, Islamic laws have evolved and changed, but the main sources of law have remained the same.

Islam imposes five practices on its followers:

- *The declaration of faith: Muslims state that there is no God but Allah and that Muhammad is the messenger of God*
- *Prayer: Muslims pray five times a day—at dawn, noon, mid-afternoon, sunset, and nightfall—reciting verses from the Quran. They may congregate at a mosque or pray at home or at their place of work.*
- *Almsgiving: Muslims make donations to charity every year.*
- *Fasting: Muslims abstain from food and other worldly pleasures from dawn to dusk during the month of Ramadan.*
- *The pilgrimage to Mecca: every adult Muslim who is physically and financially able is expected to make this pilgrimage once in their lifetime.*

SHIA VERSUS SUNNI

The main difference between the Shia and Sunni sects of Islam is that Sunni Muslims recognize the claim of successors, or caliphs, who were not related to the Prophet Muhammad, while Shia Muslims do not acknowledge this claim.

The rift between the Sunni and Shia groups formed early in Islamic history. One of the chief points of argument was what to do after the death of the Prophet Muhammad in 632 CE. The Shia Muslims of Persia argued that only Muhammad's son-in-law, Ali, had the right to be regarded as the lawful heir and successor and to rule the Muslim community after Muhammad's death.

However, there were some Muslims who opposed this claim, and the strongest opponents became the first Sunni Muslims. A Sunni caliphate was established, and the Sunni Arabs conquered new territory and expanded over time, gaining new converts along the way.

Today, some 90 percent of all Muslims belong to the Sunni branch of Islam. Shia Islam, though, is the national religion of Iran. While other points of contention evolved between Sunni and Shia Muslims over time, the original dispute is one of the biggest differences.

Another major development in Islam was the controversial religious

Three mullahs sit together outside a mosque.

mysticism called Sufism that began in the ninth century. Sufi Muslims seek to enter into very close union with God through ecstatic worship.

THE RELIGIOUS AUTHORITIES

There are many scholarly titles for people who study Islam. Among them are the *ayatollah* (AY-yah-toh-lah), *mullah* (MOO-LAH), and *ulema* (uh-LAH-mah). They, and other levels of Islamic authorities, have become unchallenged political, social, and spiritual leaders. These clerics are usually experts in Islamic studies. The ayatollahs are high-ranking Shiite religious authorities, the mullahs tend to be local Islamic clerics or mosque leaders, and the ulema are legal scholars. Applying the teachings of Islam in the fast-changing world of the twenty-first century brings many new challenges, such as addressing the relevance of religion to modern life and how one can remain true to one's religion in the face of significant social and economic changes.

THE IMPACT OF RELIGIOUS LAWS

After the Islamic Revolution of 1979, the government banned imported meat, luxury goods, and alcohol. In the 1980s music was condemned as a seducer, a distraction from serving God, and cinemas were shut down. Under religious laws, any behavior or deed that is regarded as morally dangerous has stiff penalties imposed upon it. For instance, alcohol consumption, drug abuse, and homosexuality are punishable by death. So are adultery and sex between unmarried people. In spite of this, Iranian film and theater flourished in the late 1990s and some Western musical instruments were allowed into Iran.

Not all Iranians agree with these rules. However, Islam has brought about one unity in Iranian life—all work stops when it is time to pray. Shia Islam in Iran underwent a profound transformation in the 1960s. As it became a

The Baha'i religion originated in Iran in the nineteenth century. It was started by an Iranian religious visionary, Mirza Ali Muhammad, who called himself Bab, *meaning "gate." His follower, Mirza Husain Ali (1817–92), was responsible for spreading the movement and gathering more believers. He took the title* Baha Ullah *(BAH-HAH oo-LAH), meaning "Glory of God."*

Baha'i worshipers believe that the Baha Ullah is the latest in a series of divine manifestations that include Jesus, Muhammad, Zoroaster, and the Buddha.

In the Baha'i faith, there are no initiation ceremonies, sacraments, or clergy. Every Baha'i worshiper is required to pray daily, fast for nineteen days a year, abstain from drugs and alcohol, and practice monogamy. And a Baha'i couple needs their parents' consent before marriage.

To Muslims, Baha'i believers are traitors to the "true faith." The Baha'i believe that the Messiah has already come. They criticize some of Muhammad's teachings as outmoded, such as the legal inequalities of the sexes and of creeds, polygamy, and the prejudice against music. The Baha Ullah taught that religious truth is not absolute but relative and that each age has to modify and adapt the teachings through new wisdom.

The Baha'i religion was introduced to the Western world in the 1890s. Since then Baha'i temples have been built in the United States, Germany, Australia, Panama, and Uganda. The international Baha'i governing body is known as the Universal House of Justice. It is located in Haifa, Israel, and serves as the supreme administrative, legislative, and judicial body of the Baha'i commonwealth.

The Baha'i faith has not been tolerated in Iran, particularly since the revolution. The religion has been prohibited and fought in every way. Despite the persecution, the Baha'i are still the largest religious minority living in Iran today.

political force that eventually helped to overthrow the last shah, it became more than a religious belief, but also a way of life.

WOMEN AND ISLAM

Although Islam teaches that men and women be treated equally, in practice this does not happen. In Iran millions of women participated in the revolution,

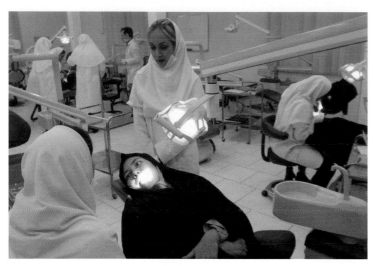

Female dentistry students, wearing white Islamic garb, practice at Tehran's Azad University.

contributing to its success. But in the aftermath, Khomeini introduced strict laws that greatly curtailed their freedom. For instance, within the family, women had no rights over their children and no protection against domestic violence.

In the 1990s women formed many groups pushing for greater rights in education, work, and marriage. Rising literacy levels since the revolution have helped women to see that there are options. Many Iranian women now work outside the home, such as in teaching and medicine, and nearly half of university students are women. However, laws segregate them so that they can only deal with other women.

Despite the growing participation of women in public life, there are considerable obstacles to further reform. For example, in 2001, when the parliament voted to give Iranian women the same rights as men to study abroad, the conservative Council of Guardians rejected the proposal. The conservatives have also arrested some women's rights activists.

OTHER RELIGIONS AND SECTS

The Ghulat are an extremist Shia sect present not only in Iran but also in Iraq, Syria, and Turkey. The Ghulat go by several names: *Ahl-i Haqq* (ahl-e HACK), or truth worshipers; *Ali Ilahis* (Ah-li ihl-AH-his), or deifiers of Ali; and *Ahl-i Allah* (ahl-e AW-LAW), or people of God. As a sect they are very secretive. Their ceremonies are conducted at night in secluded surroundings, a practice dictated at times by the need to avoid persecution. But this has given rise to all sorts of myths about their rituals and beliefs. They meet on Thursday nights and on the first night of the lunar moon, and they make public and private confessions.

One visible difference from mainstream Shia is the importance of the moustache. It is said that when the chief disciple, Ali, received instructions from the Prophet Muhammad, he knelt at Muhammad's feet, and his moustache brushed against Muhammad's body. Thus Ali's moustache acquired holiness, and, in allegiance to Ali, no Ghulat today ever clips his moustache.

There are also small numbers of Christians, Jews, and Zoroastrians in Iran. They no longer play a great political or cultural role.

Most Christians in Iran, around 300,000 of them, are members of the Armenian Church. Their largest community is in the Jolfa district at Isfahan. Christians here have their own cathedral, called the Saint Savior Cathedral, where they are allowed to celebrate Sunday Mass. Another Armenian religious center in Iran is the Saint Thaddeus the Apostle Church in Azarbayjan-e Gharbi province. Thousands of Christian pilgrims come here every July. The inhabitants of the region form a community quite firmly set apart from the rest of Iran in language and religion.

Jews in Iran number around 20,000. Many Jews left Iran after the revolution. There are ancient Jewish communities in Iran that have not changed much in their customs since Babylonian times.

INTERNET LINKS

iranprimer.usip.org/resource/iran-and-islam
Iran Primer: "Iran and Islam"
An overview of the theocracy in Iran and the role of Islam in politics and society.

www.religionfacts.com/islam/index.htm
Religion Facts: "Just the facts on religion" offers a full overview of Islam .

www.wiley.com/WileyCDA/Section/id-814560.html
TED Studies: Religion - Understanding Islam
A series of TED talks in video about Islam and Muslim life.

LANGUAGE

An example of the wedge-shaped cuneiform writing is found in an inscription in Persepolis.

9

PERSIAN IS THE OFFICIAL LANGUAGE of Iran; Persian is spoken mostly in Iran, and most Iranians speak Persian. However, there are significant populations of Persian speakers in other Persian Gulf countries—Bahrain, Iraq, Oman, People's Democratic Republic of Yemen, and the United Arab Emirates—as well as large communities in the United States. (Many Iranians who fled the country after the 1979 revolution settled in America, particularly in California.)

Although it is written in an Arabic script, the Persian language is not related to Arabic. It is spoken by an estimated 110 million people worldwide.

Linguists have identified three forms of the Persian language: Old Persian, spoken and written by the Achaemenids between the sixth century BCE and third century CE; Middle Persian, used by the Sasanids between the third and tenth centuries CE; and New Persian, used since the tenth century and today the language of not only Iranians but also peoples in Afghanistan and Tajikistan.

The name of the language and of the people comes from Pars (Fars in Arabic), an area in the southwest of the Iranian highlands. The

A statue of the beloved poet Ferdowsi stands in Ferdowsi Square in Tehran.

ancient Greeks referred to it as Persis. The people called themselves Irani, the Persian name for Aryan.

Persian is an Indo-European language; it belongs to a large family of languages that includes English, German, and French. It is not related to Turkish or Arabic, even though the language is written in Arabic script.

NEW PERSIAN

New Persian is the oldest literary language known in the region. Since the ninth century, New Persian has been written using the Arabic alphabet. The written form is very different from the spoken form and is mastered largely by the well-educated. It has remained basically unchanged since the tenth or eleventh century and is based on the renowned Iranian epic *Shahnameh*, or Epic of Kings, written by one of Persia's greatest poets, Ferdowsi. The Shahnameh consists of nearly 60,000 couplets, or pairs of rhyming lines of verse, that narrate the history of Iran.

Arabic calligraphy is written and read from right to left. Many of the letters are flowing and circular and look very attractive. Arabic motifs are abundant in Iran, where the influence of Islam dictates that all works of art be created for the glory of God.

The Persian language was very important in the past. While the first classics of literature were recorded in the tenth and eleventh centuries, the Persian language flourished well beyond Persian borders in the seventeenth century, largely due to the efforts of Shah Abbas. Under him, the empire grew in geographic dimensions and political importance. Since Persia was a world power and a conquering empire, its language became the medium of diplomacy in the entire Middle Eastern and Arab world. Persian also became the language of culture and was spoken in Cairo, Baghdad, across India, and at the court of the Turkish sultan in Istanbul.

With the fall of the Persian Empire came a decline in the use of its

language. But even today, Persian is understood as far as central Asia and India. There are Persian speakers such as the Hazara in parts of Afghanistan, including Kabul and Herat. The language is also used by the Tajik people of Tajikistan. Related literary languages are Kurdish and Baluchi dialects.

An Afghan refugee child takes a class in Persian language at a school in Pakistan.

OTHER SPOKEN LANGUAGES

Apart from the national and official language, Persian, spoken by more than half the population, there are other languages and dialects used by smaller groups of Iranians. These include some 16 million Azeri in the northwest, whose language (also called Azeri) belongs to the Turkic language group; around 4.5 million Kurds mostly in the northwest and west, who speak a variety of Kurdish dialects collectively known as Kirmanji; and about 2 million Arabs along the Persian Gulf coast, who speak Arabic, a Semitic language. Another Semitic language, used by a very small minority in Iran, is Assyrian.

There are also more than a million Lur in southwestern Iran and a similar number of Baluchi in the southeast, who speak languages of the same names.

ENGLISH WORDS DERIVED FROM PERSIAN

English is a language that has borrowed freely from many other languages over the centuries. Since both English and Persian are Indo-European languages, they share many word forms that have roots in a common origin. Linguists who trace the history and evolution of languages use the term Proto-Indo-European to mean the ancient ancestor language of a certain family of languages that spread from India to Europe. Some examples are the Persian words madar, *"mother," and* padar, *"father."*

However, English has many words that were plucked from Persian, either directly or through intermediary languages such as Greek. For example, the word paradise comes from a Persian word meaning "beautiful garden," or "walled garden," by way of the Greek paradeisos.

Other English words that have Persian origins include:

English	Persian
bazaar	bazar
jasmine	yasmin
pistachio	pistah
lilac (color)	nilak
spinach	esfenaj
sugar	shekar
shawl	shal
candy	qand (sugar)
pajama	jāmah
magic	magus (sorcerer)

(also the source of magi, the Zoroastrian priests)

Like Persian, both Lur and Baluchi belong to the Indo-European family of languages.

Like many major languages around the world, Persian is evolving as technological and scientific breakthroughs create new vocabulary.

BODY LANGUAGE

Iranians are a very expressive people, perhaps more so than people are in some Western cultures. Iranians move their hands whether they are excited or exasperated, and emotions of anger, joy, surprise, and pain show readily on their faces. When Iranians want to befriend you, they may hold out their arms toward you.

There are a few Iranian body and hand gestures that differ in meaning from the same gestures in Western countries. For example, what does it mean when a man turns his hand up and waves toward himself? In Western cultures, this might simply indicate to the other person to "come here," but in Iran such a gesture, if directed toward a woman, has suggestive motives.

Many of these gestures are influenced by social conventions and religion. Among signals of aggression, the simplest yet most offensive is the thumbs-up. It sends the recipient an insulting message. In direct contrast, the thumbs-up is a positive gesture in the United States, meaning that things are okay, that a job was well done, or that something unusual has been achieved, or it may mean good luck.

While Iranians may be very expressive in their everyday interaction with friends and family members, they are much more formal in larger social spheres than people are in the United States. One barrier lies in gender differences—a major rule in Iran is that men and women should not touch each other. Status differences are also more apparent in Iranian society.

INTERNET LINKS

www.farsinet.com/farsi
Farsinet has an excellent map of the linguistic composition of Iran.

www.omniglot.com/writing/persian.htm
Omniglot is an online encyclopedia of writing systems and languages.

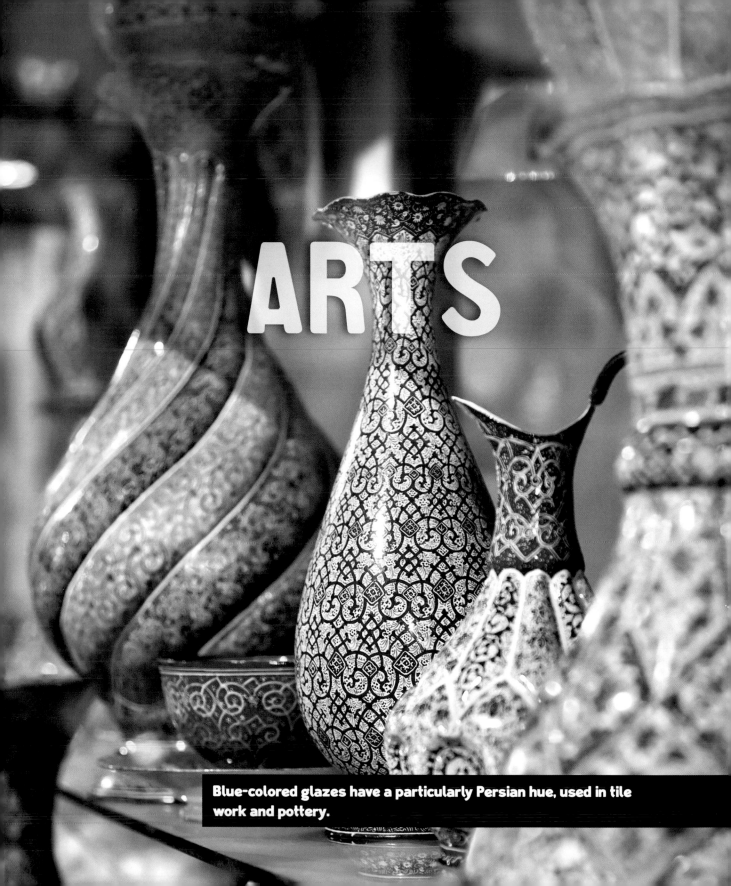

ARTS

Blue-colored glazes have a particularly Persian hue, used in tile work and pottery.

10

PERSIAN LITERATURE, ESPECIALLY poetry, is rich and varied. Persian poets have produced classics that are influential even today and that have attracted the attention of non-Iranians as well. Carpet weaving has almost reached perfection, making the name Persia synonymous with exquisite carpets.

A statue of a two-headed griffin, an ancient magical beast, stands in Persepolis.

Following the 1979 revolution, hard-line Shiite Muslim clerics banned almost all forms of music in Iran. The role of music in Islam continues to be a matter of great debate among the clerics. Under President Hassan Rouhani, some restrictions have been eased, with certain classical and traditional forms being allowed. However, TV broadcasts showing the playing of instruments are still banned. Western pop and rock music, and female solo singers, are completely off limits.

LANDSCAPE GARDENING

The renowned gardens of Naranjestan, in Shiraz, surround an opulent pavilion built in the late 1800s.

The art of landscape gardening probably had its origins in Persia. Cyrus the Great built the world's oldest known garden. It was a carefully planned garden with a pavilion and pools and canals producing the sound of flowing water and providing a soothing background for majestic trees.

Two of the most important trees used by early Persian gardeners were the plane and cypress. The most popular flowering plants were roses, in all their glorious colors, and jasmine, which gives a sweet fragrance. Fruit trees and vines, such as figs, dates, grapes, peaches, pears, and pomegranates, were also planted to beautify gardens.

Iran's landscaped gardens mimic the Qur'anic vision of paradise as a perfect garden with many shady trees, abundant fruit, scented flowers, and rippling water. Shiraz is one of Iran's most beautiful cities, with tree-lined boulevards and landscaped gardens.

HAFEZ THE POET

Iran's culture is full of poets, both past and present. One of the most famous is Hafez. Hafez was born sometime between 1310 and 1325 CE in the city of Shiraz. His full name was Khwajeh Shams al-Din Muhammad Hafez-e Shirazi. His father is said to have been a seller of coal. According to legend, as a young boy Hafez listened to his father recite the Qur'an, and memorized the entire book.

In his twenties, Hafez became a poet at the court of a local ruler. His short poems, called ghazals, *are noted for their beauty and expression of a mystical union with God. Many of his poems are used as proverbs or sayings. He has been compared to Shakespeare and other world-famous poets. Here is one of his poems:*

> The rose is not fair without the beloved's face,
>
> Nor merry the Spring without the sweet laughter of wine;
>
> The path through the fields, and winds from a flower strewn place,
>
> Without her bright check, which glows like a tulip fine,
>
> Nor winds softly blowing, fields deep in corn, are fair.
>
> And lips like to sugar, grace like a flower that sways,
>
> Are naught without kisses many and dalliance sweet;
>
> If thousands of voices sang not the rose's praise,
>
> The joy of the cypress her opening bud to greet,
>
> Nor dancing of boughs nor blossoming rose were fair.

—From Divan of Hafiz, *translated by Gertrude Lowthian Bell, (1897)*

Hafez died in 1390. His beautiful tomb, called the Hafezieh, is located in the Musalla Gardens on the banks of the Ruknabad River in Shiraz, the city of his birth.

POETRY

Some people say Persian is a particularly lovely language that is well-suited to poetry. Traditional Persian literature is almost exclusively poetry, and the poems have various forms. Some types are long odes, often of a religious nature; others tell heroic or romantic stories through narrative verse. Some types of poetry are distinguished by their forms, with certain meters, or beats, and certain numbers of stanzas, or lines of verse. Persian poetry always rhymes (in Persian), but it is very difficult to translate into English. One reason is that the poetry of Persia depends a great deal on the beauty of language for its effects.

Some of the greatest Persian poets are Ferdowsi, Omar Khayyam, Anvari, Rumi, Saadi, and Hafez.

EARLY ARCHITECTURE

The Greek historian Herodotus wrote in detail about early Persian architecture. He gave the world fascinating descriptions of early Persian cities and

An ancient mud village in the desert

buildings. Most of these structures were made of brick. There were descriptions of fire temples with fire altars, reflecting the religious beliefs of the early Persians. There were also palaces with fortresses.

Abstract decoration was a major feature of Persian architectural style, especially after the Islamic period. Bricks were laid in a decorative manner, sometimes in high relief, sometimes inset. The effect was an amazingly intricate geometric pattern. Glazed colored tilework was also used to enhance the decorative brickwork.

MOSQUES

The Arab invasion of Iran brought an Islamic influence on Persian architecture, especially between 641 and 1000 CE. The Islamic house of worship, the mosque, was essentially a large open structure with arcades and a sheltered sanctuary. Inside, a prayer niche directed worshipers to face Mecca, Islam's holiest city, when they prayed. The mosque also had a minaret from which the faithful were called to prayer. The dome was the most important feature of the mosque. It was built over the principal chamber of the mosque. Because of their awe-inspiring shape, domes took on a symbolic religious significance, and as the years went by the domes became larger in diameter and rose higher and higher. Many of the domes were covered in special blue tiles that sparkled in the sun for all to see. Persian architects also designed methods of erecting domes and vaults without using any supporting columns.

The Shah Mosque in Isfahan exemplifies the exquisite tilework often used on Iran's sacred buildings.

The interiors of many historic buildings, such as the Sultan Amir Ahmad historic bath in Kashan, are intricately decorated.

The elements remain the same for today's mosques, whether they are architecturally traditional or modern in style. Indeed, mosques old and new display the ultimate achievements of the Islamic arts in their spectacular arches, domes, minarets, and intricately-designed tilework.

Although Iran's mosques are splendid examples of Islamic Persian architecture, many of the nation's beautiful baths, bridges, palaces, and shrines were also built by Persian architects in the Islamic period.

PAINTING

There are three main features of traditional Persian painting: they are highly stylized, often using abstractions; they are colorful; and they are idealistic. Persian painters are known for their imaginative rendering of flowers, plants, and animals on almost any surface of any size.

Early Persian painting was mostly confined to books. Illustrated books became works of art during the Safavid period, with myths and legends as the favorite subjects for miniature painters. (Many Persian carpet weavers often used figures from miniature paintings, which they enlarged in their carpet designs.)

Early Persian painters rarely signed their names to their work. Hence, unlike the early European painters, very little is known about the pioneers of early Persian painting.

Traditional painters tended to portray an enchanted world of perfection. However, since 1979 the trend in Iranian painting has been to move away from the ideal to more realistic representations. While early paintings depicted kings and their activities, modern paintings show ordinary people in everyday situations. Present-day Iranian painters use their imagination in a wider sense to express different emotions, from joy to sorrow.

Despite the limitations of life in Iran, many women find self expression and fulfillment in education and the arts.

PERSIAN MINIATURE PAINTING

One of Iran's best known visual art forms, aside from Persian carpets, is Persian miniature painting. These small works of paint on paper are mainly illustrations dating to medieval times. Since the primary literature of Persia was poetry, the illustrations were usually created to decorate manuscripts of poems. The artistry of both forms worked together.

The art of miniature painting reached its peak in Persia during the era of Mongol rule, from the thirteenth to the sixteenth centuries. The Mongol invaders brought a large number of Chinese artists to Persia, and their influence can be seen in the Persian paintings.

Although styles would change over the centuries, Persian miniatures are characterized by bright, pure colors, lavish use of gold, and intricately patterned backgrounds. Colors are often used according to their symbolic meanings, and many paintings have exquisitely decorated borders. The scenes are flat, with no perspective, and the people are drawn simply. Nevertheless, the bold compositions are full of visual rhythms, elegant grace, balance, and harmony.

In other Islamic cultures, portraying the human figure was—and still is—forbidden. But Persian Muslims took a different view, and the paintings are full of people. The paintings tell stories of legends, heroic battles, human tragedies, courtly life, and love.

CERAMIC ARTS

The potter's art has existed since 6000 BCE in Iran. Several distinctive examples of ancient pottery have been found in the province of Khorasan. These are mainly flat bowls with a colorless glaze over brightly colored designs.

Other ancient Iranian vessels that have been unearthed include jugs and jars in the shape of various animals such as deer and goats. Archaeologists have also uncovered numerous artifacts that are mainly stone carvings of animals and human heads. There are also small animal figures in bronze and other precious metals.

Potters in Iran produced exquisite works during the Islamic period as well. They made earthen utensils, which they painted in many colors and decorated with the images of animals and plants using three techniques: engraving, molding, and embossing.

A craftsman engraves a brass jar using the same techniques that have existed for centuries.

CALLIGRAPHY

Calligraphy is a special art of writing that is held in great esteem in the Islamic world. God's messages were in Arabic, so Muslims consider the Arabic script sacred and the task of copying out the whole or parts of the Qur'an in beautiful writing a meritorious act. Many calligraphers enjoy great prestige because of the association of this art form with the Qur'an.

CARPETS

Persian carpets are famous all over the world. They are designed not only to be comfortable to sit or sleep on, but also as works of art for display in the home.

The Islamic emphasis on geometry and straight lines is not common in Persian carpet designs. Instead, curling flowers and tendrils are more common. Although most Islamic countries banned any artistic representation of living creatures, Iran rejected this ban and Iranian artists used human and animal figures quite frequently in their carpet designs. Traditional Persian carpets of the sixteenth and seventeenth centuries were adorned with the images of tweeting birds and sweet-smelling flowers, portraying a beautiful garden to remind them of paradise.

The color or dye used in carpet making is all-important. Traditionally, dyes were made from plants or insects. In Persian culture, colors have symbolic meanings: white for death, mourning, and grief; black for destruction; orange for devotion and piety; red for happiness and wealth; and brown for fertility.

Original handmade Persian carpets fetch very high prices in foreign markets. Each of these carpets has a unique character that cannot be reproduced exactly, not even by the same artist. Cheaper carpets that are

THE MOST EXPENSIVE CARPET IN HISTORY

The legend behind the carpet of Chosroes II describes the lengths its makers went to in producing the most expensive carpet in history:

Chosroes II was a Sassanid ruler who loved the arts. He commissioned an exquisite carpet for his palace at Ctesiphon, then the capital of Persia. The design for the carpet was astonishing in its realism. It depicted an enormous garden with flowerbeds, trees, and stones. Pure gold and silver threads represented sparkling streams, and precious gems were inlaid to enhance the illusion of springtime. Thus the king could see the colors of spring whenever he entered the room no matter the season.

Unfortunately, the most expensive carpet in history did not last long. When Arab invaders overthrew the Sassanian dynasty, they are said to have cut the carpet into pieces and taken the jewels as part of their war booty.

Ruins of Ctesiphon

mass-produced in factories may imitate original patterns but can never match handmade carpets in their quality and design.

This traditional art of handweaving carpets is a treasure to be passed on from generation to generation. However, many younger Iranians are reluctant to take up this art, preferring the excitement of city life instead. Yet carpet weaving remains the most widespread handicraft in Iran.

Iranian musicians Mohammad Ghavihelm and Mohammad Reza Lotfi play the daf, a handheld drum, and a sitar, a three-stringed lute, in a concert in New York City.

IRANIAN MUSIC

Traditionally, musicians in Iran never enjoyed a high social position, although they would play at special events such as weddings and circumcision ceremonies. Stringed instruments often accompanied the singers. Vocals sung with improvisation are a very important aspect of traditional Iranian music. The songs are often mournful.

Folk music is played in the villages when people celebrate a festival or special family event. Male dancers entertain, sometimes dressed as females. Traditional musicians and groups such as Boushehr's Leymer Folk Music Group perform at annual festivals such as the Fajr Music Festival, usually held in February, and the Iranian Epic Music Festival, usually held in April.

A special type of music is performed in the traditional wrestling establishment called *Zur Khaneh* (ZOOR KAH-nah), or "House of Power." Drums provide vigorous background music to which verses of poems such as

Ferdowsi's *Shahnameh* are sung, as the gymnasts perform feats of strength with heavy paddles.

The ability to recite the Qur'an is greatly admired. Iranian children are taught at an early age to recite verses from the Qur'an, and when they grow older, they are encouraged to take part in Qur'an-reading performances or competitions. These are often held in the fasting month of Ramadan.

Iranians still play many traditional musical instruments. Some of the more popular ones are the sitar, a lute; the *santur* (san-TOOR), a seventy-two-stringed instrument; the *kamenchay* (kah-men-CHAY), a spike-fiddle; the *zarb* (ZAHRB), a goblet-shaped drum; and the *nay* (NAY), a flute. The sitar, popular in northern India, has its origins in Iran.

INTERNET LINKS

www.iranchamber.com
The Iran Chamber Society offers excellent articles on Iranian history, arts, and culture.

www.pbs.org/wgbh/pages/frontline/tehranbureau/art-house
PBS *Frontline*'s Tehran Bureau's Art House section offers many articles about arts, culture, and everyday life in Iran.

www.tehrantimes.com/arts-and-culture
The *Tehran Times* is Iran's English language newspaper.

www.tourismiran.ir
Tourism Iran, official website. Click on English.
Beautiful photographs of arts, crafts, and architecture, as well as musical audio. Select art and culture, handicrafts, or folk music.

LEISURE

Children have fun at Eram Park, a theme park in Tehran.

11

THE CONCEPT OF LEISURE IN IRAN

differs somewhat from that in other countries. History, religion, and geographical location have helped to create a diverse and varied way of life that is uniquely Iranian.

Iranians gladly open their homes to strangers and offer their guests as much as they can afford. The home is the center of all pleasurable activities and the place to go for the best Iranian cooking. A meal at home with family and friends is often a leisure activity in itself. Iranians

No tables and chairs here – a fancy restaurant in Isfahan serves meals in the traditional Iranian style, with customers sitting on carpets.

usually linger over their meals, discussing their daily affairs.

Tea drinking is a common social activity, since alcohol has been banned in Iran since the Islamic Revolution of 1979. (Islam prohibits the consumption of liquor.) In place of liquor, and for cultural reasons, tea has become a popular social drink, and the samovar is always on the boil in Iranian homes. Tea drinking carries deeper social meaning in Iran than in many other countries.

Listening to the radio and watching television are favorite pastimes, even more popular than reading a book. Iranians also while the time away by the sea, enjoying the breeze as they recall the good old days.

TRADITIONAL SPORTS

Horse racing, a sport that goes back centuries, is still a major leisure pursuit in the Iranian countryside today. Although falconry and hunting are not as common as they once were, there are Iranians who continue to train eagles or hawks for the sport of falconry.

Polo and Iranian-style wrestling are other ancient sports that continue

Nomads take part in a horse-racing event for women in the village of Qaleh Joghd.

to attract many enthusiasts in present-day Iran. Soccer and wrestling are popular spectator sports, while polo tends to have a larger following among wealthier Iranians.

MODERN SPORTS

Iranians had almost no access to modern competitive sports until World War I. When Christian missionaries visited the Middle East, they brought with them Western-style sports. Iranians then

Children play soccer near some ruins in Kerman.

began to take an interest in athletics, tennis, basketball, and swimming. Soldiers also encouraged these sports during the two world wars. Soccer became extremely popular, and today children have taken to the sport, kicking a ball in a group along the tree-lined streets of Iran.

Tennis and squash are also popular with Iranians. Squash is a more recent entrant; it is favored by urban Iranians who want to work up a sweat after a long day in the air-conditioned office. Many squash courts have been built to cater to this growing demand.

Gymnastics is actively encouraged in schools, while in the coastal regions more affluent Iranians have taken up sailing.

As in many areas of life, women have limited access to the world of sports in Iran. Only in recent years have women been allowed to attend soccer matches in the major cities. Also, women can carry out their sporting activities only in stadiums or other sporting venues that are specially designated for women. Women also have to follow strict rules about clothing, even in sports.

In spite of these restrictions, some Iranian women have become accomplished athletes. Although they are still not allowed to participate in competitions, they do represent their nation in an all-female Islamic games meet held every year.

THE HOUSE OF POWER

The House of Power, or Zur Khaneh as it is known in Iran, is believed to have originated during the Arab invasion of Persia. The House of Power started out as a secret society of young men who swore to drive out the foreign invaders.

Zur Khaneh traditions continue in present-day Iran. Members go through vigorous physical training, doing strenuous exercises to the accompaniment of drumbeats and the chanting of verses from an ancient text. The strong men wield heavy clubs, juggling them around with great speed and dexterity.

A House of Power has one large room containing a wrestling pit. There is a platform for the drummer and a space for spectators. The men wear colorful knee-length trousers. Each session ends with a wrestling match in both traditional and modern European styles.

LEISURE IN THE COUNTRYSIDE

Iranians in the villages make their own entertainment. Their leisure activities are often an extension of their work, so taking joy in their daily activities become an important part of working for a living.

Most children in Iran's villages help their parents with chores around the house or on the farm during much of the day and take a break in the evening, playing simple traditional games that they have learned from their parents and grandparents, or simply kicking a ball around. Growing up in a clan community, village children enjoy a lot of contact with same-age cousins and friends.

Traveling troupes are another source of entertainment in the Iranian countryside. A traveling group of actors occasionally goes around the villages reading poetry or performing plays about Iran's past. They tell stories of battles won and lost, of heroes in history.

Snake charmers were once common in the countryside, where people could earn a living by hypnotizing snakes with pipe tunes. Watching a snake charmer is now a rare form of entertainment, perhaps because of the draw of modern media such as radio and television.

Most Iranian villages have a mosque, where many people gather for prayers on Fridays. The mosque is a focal point in the community, and worshippers usually socialize after the prayers. Sometimes people go to bathhouses to bathe and relax. Bathhouses are built underground at the source of a hot water spring.

LEISURE IN THE CITIES

The intense heat in summer compels many Iranians to focus their outdoor leisure in the relative cool of the evening and morning.

Like cafégoers in other parts of the world, people in Iran's modern cities enjoy watching the world go by from their seat in a teahouse called a *kafekhanna* (KAH-FEEK-hah-nah), which actually means coffeehouse.

It is common to see people drinking in a teahouse under a bridge in Isfahan. Teahouses are also the place to smoke a hubble-bubble pipe, or *hookah* (HOO-kah). The smoker inhales smoke through a tube attached to a jar that is partly filled with water. The water cools the smoke before it reaches the smoker's lips.

In the traditional cities, women seldom take part in leisure activities outside the home, as household chores take up much of their time. However, they do get a welcome break from the routine of everyday life with visits to

Shoppers explore the goods at the huge bazaar in Mashhad.

Iranians love to relax with the samovar and the water pipe. Both are often beautifully crafted using Persian art motifs, an indication of the importance these objects play in the Iranian culture.

__The Samovar__ The samovar is a metal, usually copper, urn used to heat water for tea. It is always on the boil in homes, teahouses, government offices, and bazaars. Many Iranians will lug a samovar with them even to a picnic, even on a hot day.

The custom of drinking tea in Iran is a relatively recent event. It was probably introduced from Russia in the nineteenth century. Before then, most Iranians were coffee drinkers, as were other Muslims in the Middle East. Tea has since replaced coffee as the national drink in Iran. Relaxing over a glass of tea is a favorite pastime. Tea not only quenches thirst but also has a relaxing effect.

Tea is seldom served in cups in Iran. Instead it is served in small glasses with plenty of sugar. There is a special way to enjoy tea too, by placing lumps of sugar on the tongue and then sipping the tea from the glass, drawing in the smell and taste of the strong tea.

__The Water Pipe__ The water pipe, or hubble-bubble pipe, also called a hookah, is an appliance used for smoking tobacco. It consists of a long hose attached to a glass jar that is partly filled with water. The jar is sometimes beautifully decorated, and the water may be flavored with fruit juice. A small dish for tobacco is fitted to the top of the jar.

Pipe smoking is a very social activity—Iranians go to teahouses in groups and take their time, carrying on long conversations. Both men and women smoke the water pipe. It is a cultural tradition not only in Iran but in other Middle Eastern countries as well. (Note: A 2005 report by the World Health Organization states that smoking a water pipe is a health hazard and not a safe alternative to smoking cigarettes.)

the bazaar or to the mosque, where they get many opportunities for social interaction. Women also enjoy entertaining friends and relatives at home or making handicrafts such as rugs.

Pastimes during winter include listening to music and, especially for wealthier people living in the bigger cities, skiing.

OTHER PASTIMES

Many Iranians love a picnic in the park. A rug and some finger food and soft drinks make for a simple outing close to nature. The outdoors can be enjoyed most of the year in the dry climate, if one can bear the heat.

Chess is a well-loved game in Iran. Iranians call the king piece *shah*. It is from this word that the word chess was derived. Similarly checkmate comes from the word *shahmat* (SHAH-mad), meaning "the king is dead," or "the king is helpless."

Religious leaders have banned chess several times because of the associated practice of gambling, forbidden under Islamic law. Despite these occasional decrees, the game always seems to make a comeback.

INTERNET LINKS

www.iranchamber.com/art/articles/brief_history_persian_carpet.php
"A Brief History of the Persian Carpet and its Patterns."

www.iranchamber.com/sport/chess/chess_iranian_invention.php
Iran Chamber Society: "Chess, Iranian or Indian Invention?"
An in-depth article on the history of chess as it relates to Persia.

www.tehrantimes.com/sports
The *Tehran Times* is Iran's English language newspaper.

FESTIVALS

A woman jumps over a bonfire during the Wednesday Fire Feast in March 2013, a celebration held in anticipation of the spring holiday of Now Ruz.

12

RELIGIOUS FESTIVALS AND holidays—and there are many in Iran—are a major part of traditional family life. Most holy days commemorate some aspect of the life and teaching of the Prophet Muhammad. Most Iranians follow a version of Islam called Shia, so they commemorate some aspects of the life and teaching of the founders and leaders of this branch of Islam.

Iranians commemorate some religious events with mourning, remembering the suffering of the early leaders of Shia Islam, such as Ali ibn Abi Talib, the Prophet's son-in-law and the only rightful successor recognized by Shia Muslims. Ali ibn Abi Talib's sons, Hussein and Hassan, also met untimely deaths and never took up leadership after their father's death.

But not all Iranian festivals are Islamic. The New Year festival of *Now Ruz* (no-ROOS) dates back to pre-Islamic days. Iranians practice ancient traditions during the season of Now Ruz, such as jumping over fires.

Then there are holidays that celebrate important political events in Iran's history since the fall of the shah. These occasions are usually celebrated with much pomp and ceremony, especially in Tehran. Street parties are also part of the celebrations during nonreligious festivals.

Christians make up less than 1 percent of Iranians, yet Christmas is gaining popularity as a holiday there among some Muslims, especially young people. Under previous, stricter regimes, all signs of Christmas were forbidden, but recently, restrictions have been relaxed. Stores sell secular Christmas decorations such as Santas and Christmas trees.

FESTIVALS OF THE PROPHET

Muslims usually celebrate the Prophet's birthday at a mosque. Special prayers are held, and sometimes a religious leader takes the opportunity to remind the worshippers of their Islamic beliefs and duties. Muslims usually spend the day quietly. At home parents may tell their children stories about Muhammad's life, his parents, and his birth.

Muslims do not commemorate the death of the Prophet in a big way. Instead they celebrate his ascension into heaven. This is called *Leilat al Meiraj* (LAY-lah ahl MEH-RAJ). It is a solemn festival, and sometimes people may visit graves.

People light candles to commemorate the death of Imam Hussein, the grandson of the Prophet Muhammad, during the observance of Ashura.

EID AL-ADHA

Every year Muslims all over the world perform a sacrificial ritual in remembrance of a holy man's faith in God and his submission to God's will. This is the celebration of *Eid al-Adha* (eed ahl-AHD-ha), or the feast of the sacrifice.

The festival of Eid al-Adha commemorates Abraham's willingness to sacrifice his son in obedience to God. Abraham is a well-known patriarch among Christians, Muslims, and Jews, who have in common the Old Testament.

The Muslim version of the event tells how Abraham was about to offer his son Ishmael as a sacrifice at Mina, near Mecca, when a voice called out to him to stop. An angel then appeared with a lamb and offered it in place of Abraham's son. Gratefully, Abraham took the animal and sacrificed it.

That is why Muslims commemmorate the event every year with the sacrifice of an animal, usually a lamb or young goat. As Muslims regard all life as sacred, they say prayers and kill the animal in a prescribed way following specific rites. The meat is distributed to the poor.

RAMADAN

Ramadan is the most sacred month in the Islamic lunar calendar. Every day at dawn during this month, Muslims begin a fast. They are allowed to eat and drink again when the last rays of the sun disappear, but they have to start their fast again at the next sunrise. Some Iranians are so strict in observing the fast that they do not even swallow their saliva during the day.

During Ramadan, an Iranian family breaks the daily fast after sundown in August 2010.

Shia Muslims observe the twenty-first and twenty-second days of the Ramadan month as days of mourning. This is in memory of the martyrdom of Ali ibn Abi Talib, the Prophet's son-in-law. During those two days, devout followers take to the streets beating their breasts and wailing.

The Ramadan month ends with the sighting of the new moon. A religious leader or an elder will usually announce the end of the fasting month. Then begins perhaps the most festive Islamic festival—Eid al-Fitr. Iranian sweets and snacks prepared during the Ramadan month are laid on decorated tables, and everyone is invited to eat as much as they want to relieve the tension of the fast.

Amid the festivities and merrymaking of Eid al-Fitr, Muslims remember the true, spiritual meaning of the event by attending community prayers held either in a mosque or in an open space. Devout Muslims will wash themselves thoroughly and put on clean clothes before going to the prayers. They will also have given alms to the poor or to needy relatives during the month of Ramadan.

When they have fulfilled their religious obligations, Muslims spend the rest of Eid al-Fitr visiting their friends and relatives and feasting on traditional dishes and desserts.

NOW RUZ

Now Ruz, the Iranian New Year, is celebrated on March 21—the first day of spring. Iranians look forward to this day, hoping for better times. In Iran, as in other countries, anticipation is part of the fun when it comes to celebrating the New Year. However, the traditional way in which Iranians celebrate differs somewhat. The month before Now Ruz is a busy time of preparation. Fifteen days before the festival begins, people plant wheat or lentil seeds in a shallow saucer at home. They herald the first day of spring when they see green shoots emerge from the seeds.

Other activities to prepare for the New Year include spring cleaning. People give their homes a thorough cleaning inside and out: carpets are dusted and sunned; curtains are taken down and washed; and new furniture might even be bought.

Everyone, rich or poor, shops for new clothes for themselves and for the less fortunate. Business people give gifts to their employees, hoping this generosity will bestow upon them good luck for future business.

Colored eggs, goldfish, and wheat or barley sprouts are some of the traditional symbols of Now Ruz.

On the thirteenth day of Now Ruz, Iranians have picnics and spend time outdoors.

Just before the New Year, in every household candles burn in each room, creating an atmosphere of joy. A special table is set aside, with a candle and mirror in the center. The Qur'an, a bowl of water with a floating leaf, fruit, and various colored items are also placed on the table. Family members gather to await the exact time signifying the new year. The movement of the leaf on the water is a special sign that Iranians view as the start of the new year. Quite often, in the larger cities and towns, a cannon is fired or a gong sounded to herald the new year.

Now Ruz celebrations go on for thirteen days; this is a period of socializing. Friends and relatives visit to wish one another happiness for the new year. Old quarrels are forgotten, and forgiveness is the main theme. Children enjoy this holiday the most, perhaps, because they get money or other gifts. Older members of the household usually stay home during the first few days to welcome guests. They set the table with traditional homemade sweets and drinks, which they actively encourage their guests to try. Visitors arrive in a continuous stream from morning to evening. The thirteenth day of the New Year is considered unlucky. In order to keep bad luck out of the house, the bowls

Shia Muslims perform a religious play during Ashura. The man in the center portrays Jesus Christ, who is regarded as a prophet in Islam.

of green shoots are thrown out, and most families go out for a picnic. An elaborate picnic lunch is packed, and everyone sets out by car or bus for some comfortable spot away from the home, hoping to chase away all the bad luck for the day. During the thirteen-day new year period, visits, gifts, and greetings are exchanged, and mounds of sweets eaten.

ASHURA

The tenth day of the month of Muharram is Ashura, the anniversary of the martyrdom of the Prophet's grandson Hussein in 680 CE at Karbala, a city in present-day Iraq. Although Muslims all over the world mourn his death, Shia Muslims consider the murder of Hussein by the army of the Umayyad caliph Yazid I a particularly dreadful crime. Thus Shia Muslims mourn Hussein's death in a public show of sorrow that lasts a whole month.

During the observance of Muharram, mourners make a procession through the streets and give themselves over to frenzied expressions of grief, flogging themselves with flails, cutting their bodies with blades, or piercing their skin with hooks. Sermons given at public places and at mosques reinforce the Prophet's teachings and highlight stories about Hussein's sufferings.

Shia Muslims also mark the tragedy at Karbala with passion plays, or *ta'ziyeh* (tah-ZHIH-yah), usually acted out in three acts: the first act deals with events before the battle; the second deals with the battle itself; and the third deals with events following the battle. To commemorate the tragic circumstances of the martyr's deaths, many well-to-do Iranians donate money and goods to the poor. Some hold feasts for the poor. There are no weddings or parties during Muharram, and red is forbidden. Some men wear black.

NATIONAL HOLIDAYS

Iran's national holidays celebrate major events in the nation's recent history. The holiday on February 11 celebrates the fall of Reza Shah. Oil Nationalization Day, on March 20, is the anniversary of Iran's assumption of control of its oil from the Western powers that had been profiting from it.

As mentioned earlier there is the Iranian New Year, called Now Ruz. This starts on March 21, and although the holidays run until March 25, visiting and feasting goes on for thirteen days.

Islamic Republic Day is a day to renounce the United States and Israel.

April 1 is not known as April Fool's Day in Iran; it is Islamic Republic Day. People come out into the streets in large numbers, carrying placards with life-size—or larger than life-size—pictures of their beloved leader, Ayatollah Khomeini. Western nations, seen as enemies of the revolution, are often targets of Iranian disapproval; this shows on placards carrying anti-Western slogans.

INTERNET LINKS

www.iranchamber.com/culture/articles/festival_of_fire.php
Iran Chamber Society: "Festival of Fire or 'Chahar Shanbeh Soori' "
An interesting story about an ancient Persian holiday festival.

www.npr.org/templates/story/story.php?storyId=88156775
NPR: "Fresh Foods Ring in Persian New Year of Nowruz"
This story discusses the foods and symbols of Now Ruz.

www.pbs.org/wgbh/pages/frontline/tehranbureau/2008/12/a-winter-trend-deck-the-halls.html
PBS *Frontline*, Tehran Bureau: "A Winter Trend: Deck the Halls"
A story about the growing popularity of Christmas in Iran.

FOOD

Rice is an important crop in Iran. This woman plants rice in a paddy field in the northwestern part of the country.

13

FOOD, GLORIOUS FOOD! THAT IS what Marco Polo probably thought when he sampled the famous melons of Persia. Iranians still grow an incredible variety of melons, and there are some street stalls that sell only melons. But apart from melons, Iranian food is often regarded as one of the most refined cuisines in the Middle East.

A special delicacy in Iran is *kaleh pacheh*, a dish of meat in a thick broth. It is made from the entire head of a sheep (including brain, eyes, and tongue) and its hooves. These parts are boiled for a long time, seasoned with lemon and cinnamon, and typically served only from 3 a.m. until dawn as a kind of breakfast soup.

A woman sells fruits and vegetables in Minab.

Workers in a bakery in Yazd make traditional flatbread, one of the most important parts of the Iranian diet.

Today Iranian cuisine is particularly well-known for its rice dishes. Nowhere in the world—except perhaps in India—do people give so much time and care to the preparation of rice dishes.

Bread is another favorite food in Iran. There is an amazing variety of unleavened breads to choose from every morning.

Authentic traditional Iranian cuisine is very old. It was born in the early days of the first Persian Empire. It has since grown in sophistication. External influences have, of course, affected the development of Iranian cuisine. Some areas in the southeast of the country serve curries, an influence from India, while the Arab influence is more evident in areas around the Persian Gulf. Turkish influence is strong near the border with Turkey and Azerbaijan.

The home is the heart of Iranian cuisine. Every homemaker has her own unique and imaginative cooking style, based on secrets that she has inherited from her mother or grandmother.

Side dishes are an essential part of Iranian cuisine; strictly speaking, Iranians do not categorize dishes as entrées and main courses. The main course of rice or bread is extended to include a wide range of side dishes, depending on the number of people sharing the meal.

MEAT AND FISH

Muslim Iranians do not eat pork, because Islam forbids it. They do not eat much beef either, because the country lacks large enough grazing lands to support sizeable herds of cattle. Lamb is the favorite meat in Iran, often slaughtered when only a few days old. In the desert, lamb is slaughtered just before a meal, then spit-roasted over an outdoor fire. For roasting, lamb is usually stuffed with a mixture of rice, almonds, currants, and pine nuts.

One of the most popular dishes in Iran is *chelo kebab* (CHEH-loh KEE-bahb). Tender boneless lamb is the traditional meat used for the kebab. Pieces of meat and vegetables are skewered on metal spikes. The meat is usually marinated in a spice-laced yogurt mixture before being cooked.

The kebabs are grilled over hot coals and served on a bed of rice with side dishes of raw onions and cucumber. Marinated chicken on a skewer is called *jujeh kebab* (jew-JEH KEE-bahb).

Fishermen pull a beluga sturgeon into their boat in the Caspian Sea. The sturgeon is valued for its eggs, or caviar.

Fish, such as trout and sturgeon, is a very popular food among Iranians in the Caspian Sea area. Iranian fishers have many stories about catching sturgeon. They claim that sturgeon can live to be a century old and can weigh over a ton.

Sturgeon roe, or caviar, is a delicacy; it is too expensive for most Iranians, and much of it is exported.

RICE AND BREADS

Rice is the most important component of the daily diet of most Iranians. Rice is relatively cheap as it is largely grown locally, mostly on the Caspian coast.

A typical meal consists of a mountain of cooked rice and small servings of vegetables, meat, or fish.

An Iranian national rice dish is *chelo* (CHEH-loh). This is plain rice, boiled and buttered. When served with a special sauce, it is called *chelo khoresh* (CHEH-loh KOO-resh). The sauce is a subtle blend of vegetables and meats, sweetened or soured by the juices of pomegranates, apples, quinces, and unripe grapes.

Polo (POH-loh) is another Iranian national rice dish; it is also known as *pilau* in the rest of the Middle East and in northern India. Polo is aromatic rice cooked with several ingredients that could include any combination of vegetables, fruit, nuts, and meats.

Although rice is still popular in Iran, the government is encouraging people to eat more bread instead, because wheat cultivation does not consume as much water as rice cultivation does. The government gives wheat farmers subsidies, making bread more affordable.

Bread shops in Iran are usually small, with a simple griddle to cook bread

Rice pilaf flavored with saffron and barberries is a popular dish in Iran.

or an oven to bake it. Iranian breads come in different shapes and sizes. There is the coarse bread called *sanggak* (sahn-GAHK), made of wholemeal flour and baked over hot stones; *naan* (nahn) is an oval-shaped pancake-like bread that is either ovenbaked or cooked over a bed of small stones (*naan sanggak* is "dimpled"). The bread seller usually delivers the different types of bread on a specially-adapted bicycle, motorcycle, or van. Bakeries stack naan in piles. Iranian bread is often sold by weight.

SIDE DISHES AND SOUPS

Vegetable side dishes vary from region to region in Iran; eggplant and spinach are very popular in most parts. Raw onions and shallots are often served with rice dishes. Stuffed vegetables called *dolmeh* (DOHL-meh) are convenient finger foods that can be taken to a picnic. Eggs are a versatile side dish; they are usually beaten together with finely chopped vegetables and herbs and made into a thick omelette that is cut into small enough pieces for the fingers

Cumin and coriander are the featured spices in *kofta*, or spicy meatballs, shown here in a tomato sauce with yogurt.

YOGURT—THE PERSIAN MILK

Yogurt was part of Iranian cuisine from the early days, when it was referred to as "Persian milk." Nearly all yogurt is homemade, and it is used widely in cooking and for general consumption. It has found its way into Iranian life in many forms, and Iranians consider it a miracle food.

Yogurt can be used to make many kinds of dishes and drinks. It is added to cold and hot soups. It is used in salads. And sometimes it is whisked with water and mint to make a wonderfully cool thirst-quencher on summer days.

Yogurt contains an enzyme that helps to break down meat tissues, tenderizing meat in a marinade. It also helps spices to penetrate deep into the meat, therefore enhancing the flavor of the meat.

Iranian yogurt is usually thick-set and tastes rich and creamy. It is made from whole milk. If the fat is extracted, as in non-fat yogurt, it becomes too watery.

Iranians claim that yogurt can cure ulcers, relieve sunburn, and even prolong one's life. Some people use yogurt as a face mask.

to manage. *Koftas* are no ordinary meatballs. They are usually made from finely minced mutton or lamb, heavily spiced with herbs and stuffed with fried onions, currants, chopped nuts, and often a boiled egg in the center.

Soups are very popular in Iran. Sometimes they are served as a meal; a worker would be satisfied with *abgoosht* (up-GOOSHT), a hearty mutton soup thickened with chickpeas. Chickpeas themselves make a side dish for bread or rice dishes. Chickpeas may be boiled after soaking in water for several hours or puréed with oil and used as a dip for breads.

IRANIAN DRINKS AND SWEETS

After a hearty meal, Iranians indulge in a wide range of fruit—quinces, pears, pomegranates, grapes, dates, apricots, peaches, and the famous Iranian melons. The fruits are usually offered sliced, sometimes sweetened with rose water, or crushed and served as a colorful sherbet.

Dried fruits glitter like jewels in a display in Tehran.

People in Shiraz enjoy *palouden* (PAO-loo-den), a rose-flavored ice drink laced with lemon juice. Rose essence and rose water are used in many dishes. The essence is extracted from a variety of special roses. The ever-popular yogurt drink (yogurt whisked with water and mint) and tea are favorites during the hot months.

Iranians have a sweet tooth, but their desserts are not as sweet as those of many other Middle Eastern countries. Iranian sweets are usually made especially for festive occasions and holidays.

Halva (HAHL-wah) and *baklava* (bahk-LAH-vah) are common throughout the Middle East and very popular in Iran. The Iranian variety of baklava is smaller and not as sweet. Halva is made of flour, shortening, sugar, and nuts.

Nuts, raisins, and preserved fruits are popular snack foods for Iranians looking for something to nibble on between meals or with a glass of strong Iranian tea.

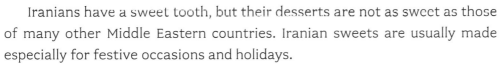

INTERNET LINKS

www.aashpazi.com
Persian recipes for American kitchens.

turmericsaffron.blogspot.com
Persian cuisine, recipes, and stories.

PERSIAN SHISH KEBAB

Makes four servings

2 pounds beef tenderloin
1 onion, chopped
1 tablespoon salt
1 pinch ground black pepper
⅛ cup fresh lime juice

Cut beef into 1-inch cubes. Place in a medium mixing bowl along with the onion, salt, black pepper, and lime juice. Mix well, cover, and refrigerate overnight.

Preheat grill for high heat. Thread beef on skewers, six to eight pieces per skewer. Lightly oil grate, and place kebab on grill. Cook for three to four minutes per side, about 12 to 16 minutes in all.

YAZDI CAKES (SHIRINI-E YAZDI)

Makes 24 cakes

2 cups all-purpose flour
1 teaspoon baking powder
1 teaspoon cardamom
4 eggs
1 ¼ cups white sugar
1 ½ cups butter, melted
1 cup plain yogurt
1 ½ teaspoons rose water
½ cup blanched slivered almonds
1 ½ tablespoons chopped pistachios

Preheat the oven to 350°F. Stir the flour and baking powder in a bowl; set aside. Grease the cups of a muffin pan, or line with paper or foil baking cups. You will need 24 cups.

Combine the eggs and sugar in a large heat-proof bowl and set on top of a pan of simmering water. Beat constantly with a whisk or electric mixer until thick and pale, about eight minutes. Remove from the heat and continue to beat until cooled, about ten minutes. Mix in the butter, yogurt, cardamom, and rose water. Stir in the flour mixture by hand and fold in the slivered almonds. Spoon into prepared muffin cups, filling them three-quarters full. Sprinkle some chopped pistachios over the tops.

Bake in the preheated oven until firm to the touch and golden brown, 25 to 30 minutes.

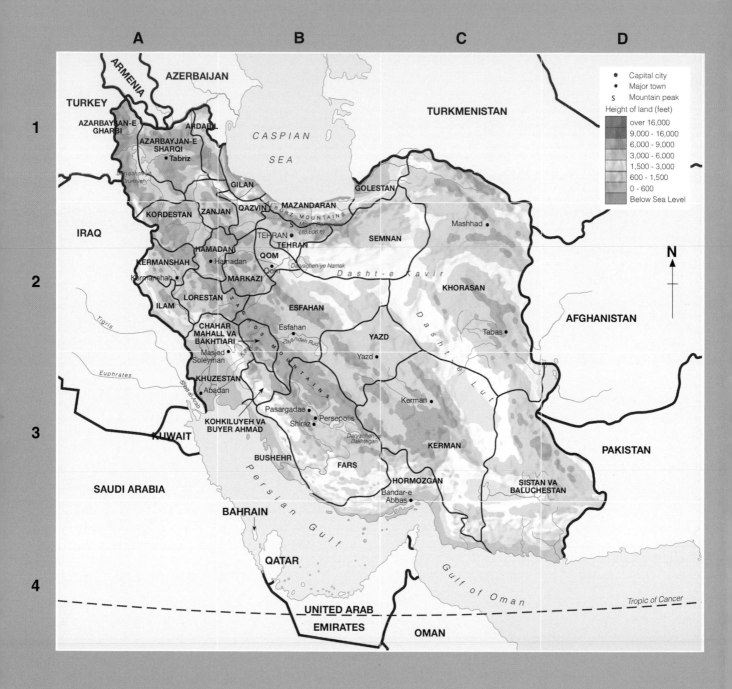

	A	**B**	**C**	**D**

1

ARMENIA

TURKEY

AZERBAIJAN

AZARBAYJAN-E
GHARBI

ARDABIL

AZARBAYJAN-E
SHARQI

• Tabriz

CASPIAN
SEA

TURKMENISTAN

GILAN

KORDESTAN

ZANJAN

QAZVIN

MAZANDARAN

GOLESTAN

IRAQ

Daryacheh-ye
Orumiyeh

BORZ MOUNTAINS

S Mount Damavand
(18,606 ft)

SEMNAN

Mashhad •

HAMADAN

TEHRAN
TEHRAN

KERMANSHAH

• Hamadan

QOM

Qom •

Daryacheh-ye Namak

Dasht-e Kavir

KHORASAN

2

Kermanshah •

MARKAZI

LORESTAN

ESFAHAN

Dasht-e Lut

AFGHANISTAN

ILAM

Tigris

ZAGROS MOUNTAINS

CHAHAR
MAHALL VA
BAKHTIARI

Esfahan •

Zayandeh Rud

YAZD

Tabas •

Masjed
Soleyman •

Yazd •

KHUZESTAN

Euphrates

Kerman •

• Abadan

Pasargadae •

Persepolis •

3

Shatt al-Arab

KUWAIT

KOHKILUYEH VA
BUYER AHMAD

Shiraz •

Daryacheh-ye
Dakhtegan

KERMAN

PAKISTAN

BUSHEHR

FARS

SAUDI ARABIA

HORMOZGAN

SISTAN VA
BALUCHESTAN

BAHRAIN

Bandar-e
Abbas •

Persian Gulf

QATAR

Gulf of Oman

4

UNITED ARAB

Tropic of Cancer

EMIRATES

OMAN

Legend:
- • Capital city
- • Major town
- S Mountain peak

Height of land (feet)
- over 16,000
- 9,000 - 16,000
- 6,000 - 9,000
- 3,000 - 6,000
- 1,500 - 3,000
- 600 - 1,500
- 0 - 600
- Below Sea Level

N

MAP OF IRAN

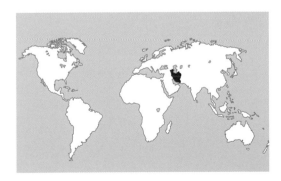

ECONOMIC IRAN

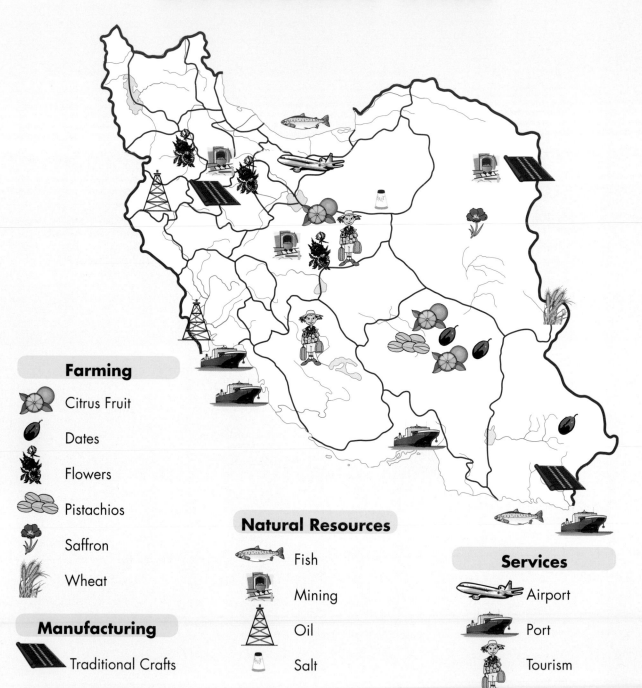

Farming

Citrus Fruit

Dates

Flowers

Pistachios

Saffron

Wheat

Manufacturing

Traditional Crafts

Natural Resources

Fish

Mining

Oil

Salt

Services

Airport

Port

Tourism

ABOUT THE ECONOMY

Iran's economy relies heavily on oil, a major source of government revenues. However, international sanctions, imposed in 2012 against the administration of President Mahmoud Ahmadinejad, significantly reduced Iran's oil revenue. They also forced government spending cuts, and fueled a 60-percent currency depreciation. Economic growth suffered a down turn in 2012 and 2013. Iran continues to experience double-digit unemployment and underemployment. Lack of job opportunities has convinced many educated Iranian youth to seek jobs overseas, resulting in a significant "brain drain." However, the election of President Hasan Rouhani in June 2013 brought about widespread expectations of economic improvements and improved international relations.

CURRENCY
Iranian rial (IRR)
Coins: 250, 500, 1000
Notes: 100, 200, 500, 1000, 2000, 10,000, 20,000, 50,000, 100,000
Iranian rials (IRR) per US dollar (2013 est.):
$1 (USD) = 24,774 rials

INFLATION RATE
42.3 percent (2013 est.)

GDP
$987.1 billion (2013 est.)

GDP SECTORS
agriculture: 10.6 percent
industry: 44.9 percent
services: 44.5 percent (2013 est.)

WORKFORCE
27.72 million

LAND AREA
total: 636, 370 sq miles (1,648,195 sq km)

LAND USE
arable land: 10 percent
permanent crops: 1 percent
other: 89 percent (2011)

AGRICULTURAL PRODUCTS
wheat, rice, other grains, sugar beets, sugarcane, fruits, nuts, cotton; dairy products, wool; caviar

UNEMPLOYMENT RATE
16 percent (2013 est.)

EXPORTS
petroleum 80 percent, chemical and petrochemical products, fruits and nuts, carpets

IMPORTS
industrial supplies, capital goods, foodstuffs and other consumer goods, technical services

MAJOR TRADE PARTNERS
UAE, China, India, Turkey, South Korea, Japan (2012)

CULTURAL IRAN

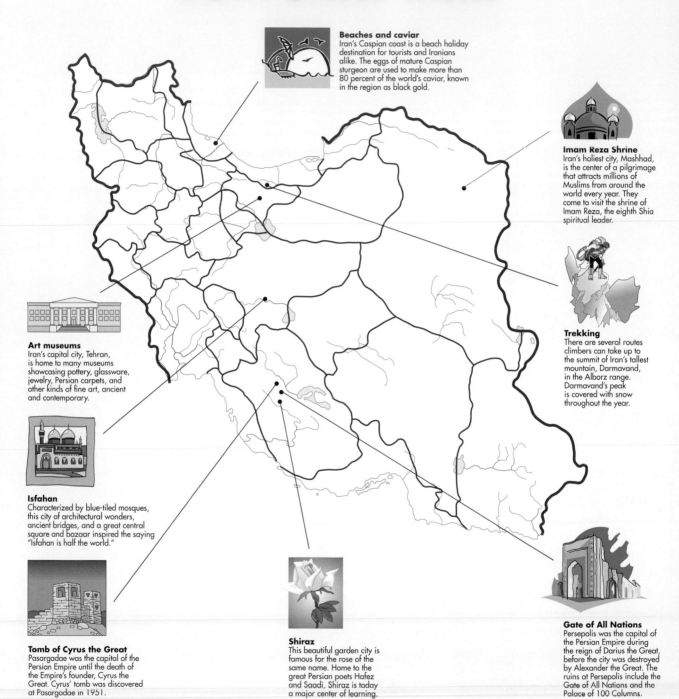

Beaches and caviar
Iran's Caspian coast is a beach holiday destination for tourists and Iranians alike. The eggs of mature Caspian sturgeon are used to make more than 80 percent of the world's caviar, known in the region as black gold.

Imam Reza Shrine
Iran's holiest city, Mashhad, is the center of a pilgrimage that attracts millions of Muslims from around the world every year. They come to visit the shrine of Imam Reza, the eighth Shia spiritual leader.

Trekking
There are several routes climbers can take up to the summit of Iran's tallest mountain, Darmavand, in the Alborz range. Darmavand's peak is covered with snow throughout the year.

Art museums
Iran's capital city, Tehran, is home to many museums showcasing pottery, glassware, jewelry, Persian carpets, and other kinds of fine art, ancient and contemporary.

Isfahan
Characterized by blue-tiled mosques, this city of architectural wonders, ancient bridges, and a great central square and bazaar inspired the saying "Isfahan is half the world."

Tomb of Cyrus the Great
Pasargadae was the capital of the Persian Empire until the death of the Empire's founder, Cyrus the Great. Cyrus' tomb was discovered at Pasargadae in 1951.

Shiraz
This beautiful garden city is famous for the rose of the same name. Home to the great Persian poets Hafez and Saadi, Shiraz is today a major center of learning.

Gate of All Nations
Persepolis was the capital of the Persian Empire during the reign of Darius the Great, before the city was destroyed by Alexander the Great. The ruins at Persepolis include the Gate of All Nations and the Palace of 100 Columns.

OFFICIAL NAME
Islamic Republic of Iran

CAPITAL
Tehran

GOVERNMENT
Theocratic republic

NATIONAL FLAG
The Iranian flag has three equal horizontal bands of green (top), white, and red. The national emblem (a stylized representation of the word Allah in the shape of a tulip, a symbol of martyrdom) in red is centered in the white band. ALLAH AKBAR ("God is Great") in white Arabic script is repeated eleven times along the bottom edge of the green band and eleven times along the top edge of the red band. Green is the color of Islam and also represents growth; white symbolizes honesty and peace; and red stands for bravery and martyrdom.

NATIONAL ANTHEM
"Soroud-e Melli-ye Jomhouri-ye Eslami-ye Iran" (National Anthem of the Islamic Republic of Iran)

POPULATION:
80,840,713 (July 2014 est.)

LIFE EXPECTANCY:
total population: 70.9 years
male: 69.3 years
female: 72.5 years (2014 est.)

LITERACY RATE:
total population: 85 percent
male: 89.3 percent
female: 80.7 percent (2008 est.)

ETHNIC GROUPS:
Persian 61 percent, Azeri 16 percent, Kurd 10 percent, Lur 6 percent, Baloch 2 percent, Arab 2 percent, Turkmen and Turkic tribes 2 percent, other 1 percent

RELIGIOUS GROUPS:
Muslim (official) 99.4 percent (Shia 90—95 percent, Sunni 5—10 percent), other (includes Zoroastrian, Jewish, and Christian) 0.3 percent, unspecified 0.4 percent (2011 est.)

NATIONAL HOLIDAYS
Fall of the Shah (February 11), Oil Nationalization Day (March 20), Now Ruz (March 21—25), Islamic Republic Day (April 1)

LEADERS IN POLITICS
Chief of state: Supreme Leader Ali Hoseini-Khamenei (since 1989)
Head of government: President Hasan Fereidun Rouhani (since 2013)
First Vice President: Eshaq Jahangiri (since 2013)

TIMELINE

IN IRAN	IN THE WORLD
2000 BCE Central Asians migrate to Iran.	
	753 BCE Rome is founded.
530–330 BCE Cyrus the Great creates the Persian Empire.	
330 BCE Alexander the Great conquers Persia.	
323 BCE Alexander dies; one of his generals forms the Seleucid dynasty.	
250 BCE Parthian invaders establish their empire.	**116–17 BCE** The Roman Empire reaches its greatest extent, under Emperor Trajan (98-17).
224 CE The Sassanids found the second Persian Empire.	**600 CE** Height of Mayan civilization
637 Arabs conquer Persia; Islam becomes the state religion.	**1000** The Chinese perfect gunpowder and begin to use it in warfare.
1051–1220 Reign of the Seljuks	
1258 Mongol invaders establish the Il-Khanid dynasty.	
1335 The Mongol dynasty falls apart; a succession of minor dynasties follows.	
1501–1722 The Safavids rule the third Persian Empire.	**1530** Beginning of trans-Atlantic slave trade organized by the Portuguese in Africa.
	1558–1603 Reign of Elizabeth I of England
	1620 Pilgrims sail the *Mayflower* to America.
1796–1925 Reign of the Qajars	**1776** U.S. Declaration of Independence
	1789–1799 The French Revolution
	1861

IN IRAN	IN THE WORLD
	1861 The U.S. Civil War begins.
	1869 The Suez Canal is opened.
	1914 World War I begins.
1926 Reza Khan founds the Pahlavi Dynasty.	
1935 Persia is named Iran.	**1939** World War II begins.
1941 British and Soviet forces invade. Reza Khan abdicates in favor of his son.	**1945** The United States drops atomic bombs on Hiroshima and Nagasaki.
	1949 The North Atlantic Treaty Organization (NATO) is formed.
	1957 The Russians launch Sputnik.
1979 The Islamic Revolution; Ayatollah Khomeini comes to power.	**1966–1969** The Chinese Cultural Revolution
1980 Iran becomes an Islamic Republic.	
1980–88 Iran-Iraq War	**1986** Nuclear power disaster at Chernobyl in Ukraine
1989 Ayatollah Khomeini dies.	**1991** Break-up of the Soviet Union
1997 Muhammad Khatami is elected president.	**1997** Hong Kong is returned to China.
	2001 Terrorist attacks on the United States
2006 UN Security council imposes sanctions on Iran.	**2003** War in Iraq
2013 Hasan Rouhani is elected president. Iran agrees to limit its nuclear program in exchange for lighter economic sanctions.	**2014** The Crimea votes to secede from Ukraine and join Russia.

GLOSSARY

ayatollah (AH-yah-toh-lah)
Title given to pious and learned religious men at the top of the Islamic Shia hierarchy

caliph
A successor of the Prophet Muhammad

chador (CHAH-dorh)
Traditional clothes worn by Iranian women in public; it covers the body from head to toe

djuba (ZHOO-bah)
A water channel

hajj
An annual pilgrimage Muslims all over the world make to Islam's holy city Mecca

halal
Permitted for consumption by Islamic law

hookah (HOO-kah)
A water, or hubble-bubble, pipe for smoking

kafekhanna (KAH-FEEK-hah-nah)
A coffeehouse turned teahouse

kamenchay (kah-men-CHAY)
A spike-fiddle

madraseh (MAH-drah-sah)
A religious school

majlis (MAHJ-liz)
An assembly of elected representatives

muezzin
A mosque official who announces prayer times

mullah (MOO-LAH)
A Muslim teacher or scholar

namak (NAH-mahk)
A shallow salt lake

nay (NAY)
A traditional Iranian flute

qanat (kah-NUT)
An underground water tunnel

samovar
A metal urn for boiling tea

santur (san-TOOR)
A traditional Iranian 72-string musical instrument

shah
A sovereign, or king, of Iran

Sufi (SOO-fi)
A follower of Sufism, or Islamic mysticism

Sunna (SOON-nah)
A guide to Islamic teaching and law that includes the sayings of the Prophet Mohammed and his answers to philosophical and legal questions

vali-ye faqih (VAH-li-yee fah-kee)
The spiritual leader of Iran; the most powerful person in the country

FOR FURTHER INFORMATION

BOOKS

Axworthy, Michael. *A History of Iran: Empire of the Mind*. New York: Basic Books, 2008.

Buchan, James. *Days of God: The Revolution in Iran and Its Consequences*. New York: Simon & Schuster, 2013.

Lumbard, Alex Yorok and Demi (illustrator), *The Conference of the Birds*. Bloomington, IN.: Wisdom Tales, 2012. (A lavishly illustrated picture book based on the thirteenth-century Sufi parable by Attar.)

Roberts, Kathrine. *I Am the Great Horse*. New York: Scholastic, 2006. (The story of Alexander the Great through the eyes of his horse.)

Rumi, Maryam Mafi and Azima Melita Kolin,(translators). *Rumi's Little Book of Life: The Garden of the Soul, the Heart, and the Spirit*. Newburyport, VA: Hampton Roads Publishing, 2012.

Satrapi, Marjane. *Persepolis: The Story of a Childhood*. New York: Pantheon, 2004.

Seidman, David. *Teens in Iran*. Mankato, MN.: Compass Point Books, 2007.

WEBSITES

Atlantic, The. "A View Inside Iran" (photo essay). January 6, 2012. www.theatlantic.com/infocus/2012/01/a-view-inside-iran/100219/

Central Intelligence Agency World Factbook (select Iran from the country list). www.cia.gov/cia/publications/factbook

Human Rights Watch (type *Iran* in the search box). www.hrw.org

Iran Chamber Society. www.iranchamber.com

Tehran Times. http://tehrantimes.com/

Tourism Iran. http://tourismiran.ir/

United States Institute of Peace. The Iran Primer. http://iranprimer.usip.org/

FILM

Kiarostami, Abbas (director). *Taste of Cherry*. Home Vision Entertainment, 1998. (DVD)

Majidi, Majid (director). *The Song of Sparrows*. E1 Entertainment, 2010. (DVD)

Majidi, Majid (director). *Children of Heaven*. Miramax, 1999. (DVD)

Panahi, Jafar (director). *The White Balloon*. Hallmark Home Entertainment, 1995. (VHS)

MUSIC

Kula Kulluk Yakisir Mi. ECM / Universal Music, 2013 (CD)

Music of the Persian Mystics. Arc Music, 2003. (CD)

Persian Classical Music. Nonesuch, 1991. (CD)

Persian Love Songs & Mystic Chants. Lyrichord Discs Inc., 1991. (CD)

Rough Guide to the Music of Iran. World Music Network. 2006. (CD)

Without You: Masters of Persian Music. World Village, 2002. (CD)

BIBLIOGRAPHY

Al Jazeera. "The Revolution That Shook the World."
aww.aljazeera.com/indepth/features/2014/01/iran-1979-
revolution-shook-world-2014121134227652609.html

Ancient History Encyclopedia. Persia. www.ancient.eu.com/Persia/

Baker, Patricia. *Iran*. Bucks, United Kingdom: Bradt Travel Guides, 2001

BBC News. "Iran Profile." Nov. 24, 2014. www.bbc.com/news/world-middle-east-14541327

Central Intelligence Agency World Factbook. Iran Country Profile. www.cia.gov/cia/publications/
factbook

Clawson, Patrick. "Iran Beyond Oil?" The Washington Institute for Near East Policy, April 3, 2013.
www.washingtoninstitute.org/policy-analysis/view/iran-beyond-oil

Del Giudice, Marguerite. "Persia: Ancient Soul of Iran." *National Geographic*, August 2008.
ngm.nationalgeographic.com/2008/08/iran-archaeology/del-giudice-text

Iran Chamber Society. www.iranchamber.com

Poetry Foundation. Hafez. www.poetryfoundation.org/bio/hafez

Wright, Martin (editor). *Iran: The Khomeini Revolution*. Countries in Crisis series. New York:
Longman, 1989.

United States Institute of Peace. The Iran Primer. http://iranprimer.usip.org/

INDEX

INDEX